CW00927970

FREE BOOKS

*www.**forgottenbooks**.org*

You can read literally <u>thousands</u> of books
for free at www.forgottenbooks.org

(please support us by visiting our web site)

Truth may seem, but cannot be:
Beauty brag, but 'tis not she;
Truth and beauty buried be.

To this urn let those repair
That are either true or fair;
For these dead birds sigh a prayer.

Bacon

Ethics and the Materialist Conception of History

By KARL KAUTSKY

Translated by JOHN B. ASKEW

FOURTH EDITION: REVISED

CHICAGO
CHARLES H. KERR & COMPANY
1918

PREFACE

Like so many other Marxist publications the present one owes its origin to a special occasion, it arose out of a controversy. The polemic in which I was involved last Autumn with the editors of Vorwärts brought me to touch on the question of their "ethical tendencies." What I said, however, on this point was so often misunderstood by one side, and on the other brought me so many requests to give a more thorough and systematic exposition of my ideas on Ethics, that I felt constrained to attempt at least to give a short sketch of the development of Ethics on the basis of the materialist conception of history. I take as my starting point, consequently, that materialist philosophy which was founded on one side by Marx and Engels, on the other, though in the same spirit, by Joseph Dietzgen. For the results at which I have arrived I alone am responsible.

My original intention only got so far as to write an article for the " Neue Zeit " on the subject. But never had I so miscalculated over the plan of a work as this time; and not only in respect of its scope. I had begun the work in October, because I thought there were now going to be a few months of quiet for the party, which might be devoted to theoretical work. The Jena Congress had run so harmoniously that I did not expect to see a conflict in our own party so soon. On the other hand it looked at the beginning of October as if there had come in the Russian revolution a pause for gathering together and organizing the revolutionary forces.

As is well known, however, everything turned out quite differently. An unimportant personal question was the occasion of a sharp discussion, which indeed did not for a moment disturb the party, but all the same cost the party officials and especially those in Berlin, a considerable amount of time, worry and energy. What, however, certainly demanded even more time and energy was the Russian revolution, which unexpectedly in the course of that very October received a powerful impetus and regained its previous height. That glorious movement naturally absorbed even out of Russia all the interest of revolutionary thinking people. It was a magnificent time, but it was not the most suitable moment to write a book on ethics. However, the subject had captivated me and I could not free myself, and so I concluded my work despite the many distractions and interruptions, which the Berlin storm in a teacup, and the hurricane in the Russian ocean brought with them. It is to be hoped that the little work does not bear too obviously on its face the marks of its stormy birth. When, however, I had brought it to a conclusion another question arose. Far beyond the limits of an article had it grown, and yet was hardly fitted for a book. It contents itself with giving a general idea of my thought, and gives very few references to facts and arguments to prove or illustrate what has been brought forward.

I asked myself whether I ought not to reconstruct and enlarge my work by the addition of such arguments and facts. If, however, that had to be done it would mean delaying the publication of the book for an indefinite period; because to carry out this work would require two years' quiet undisturbed labor. We are, however, coming to a time when for every Social Democrat quiet and undisturbed work will be impossible, where our work will be continual fighting. Neither did I desire that the publication should be put off for too long a time in face of the influence which has been won in our ranks by the ethics of Kant, and I consequently hold it necessary to show the relations which exist between the materialist conception of history and Ethics.

Consequently I have resolved to allow the little book to appear. However, to show that with this not all is said which I might have said on Ethics, and that I hold myself in reserve to deal with the subject more fully in a period of greater calm, I call the present work simply an attempt — an Essay. Certainly when these quieter times will come is not to be seen at present, as I have already remarked. At this very time the myrmidons of the Czar are zealously at work to rival the deeds of the Alvas and Tillys during the religious struggles of the sixteenth and seventeenth centuries — not in military achievements, but in brutal destruction. The west European champions of culture and order greet that with enthusiasm as the restoration of legal conditions. But just as little as the hirelings of the Hapsburgs succeeded, despite temporary successes, in conquering North Germany and Holland for Catholicism will the Cossacks of the Romanoffs succeed in restoring the rule of absolutism. This has sufficient strength remaining to lay its country waste, not to rule it. In any case the Russian Revolution is not by a long way at an end — it cannot close so long as the peasants are not appeased. The longer it lasts, so much the greater will be the disturbances in the rank of the west European proletariat, so much the nearer financial catastrophes, so much the more probable that even in west Europe there should set in a period of sharp class struggles.

That is no time which calls for the theoretical labors of revolutionary writers. But this drawback for our theoretical labors, which will probably be felt in the next few years, we need not lament. The materialist conception of history is not only important because it allows us to explain history better than has been done up to now, but also because it enables us to make history better than has been hitherto done. And the latter is more important than the former. From the progress of the practice our theoretical knowledge grows and in the progress of the practice our theoretical progress is proved. No world-conception has been in so high a degree a philosophy of deeds as the dialectical materialism. Not only upon research but upon deeds do we rely to show the superiority of our philosophy.

Even the book before us has not to serve for contemplative knowledge, but for the fight, a fight in which we have to develop the highest ethical strength as well as the greatest clearness of knowledge if we are to win.

KARL KAUTSKY.

Berlin-Friedenan, January, 1906.

TABLE OF CONTENTS

ETHICS AND THE MATERIAL IST CONCEPTION OF HISTORY

CHAPTER I

ANCIENT AND CHRISTIAN ETHICS

In the history of Philosophy the question of Ethics comes to the fore soon after the Persian wars. The repulsion of the gigantic Persian despotism had had a similar effect on the tiny Hellenic people to that of the defeat of the Russian despotism on the Japanese. At one blow they became a world-power, ruling the sea which surrounded them and with that commanding its trade. And if now over Japan the great industry is going to break with a weight of which they have only as yet experienced the commencement, so, after the Persian wars, Greece, and Athens in particular, became the headquarters of the world commerce of that time, commercial capitalism embraced the entire people and dissolved all the traditional relations and conceptions which had hitherto ruled the individual and regulated his dealings. The individual found himself suddenly transplanted into a new society — and

indeed the more so the higher he stood socially
— in which he lost all the traditional supports,
in which he found himself left wholly to himself. And yet despite all this seeming anarchy,
everyone felt not only a need for distinct rules
of conduct, but he found more or less clearly
that in his own inner being there worked a regulator of his action which allowed him to decide
between good and bad, to aim for the good and
to avoid the bad. This regulator revealed itself
as a highly mysterious power. Granted that it
controlled the actions of many men, that its decisions between good and bad were given without
the least delay and asserted themselves with all
decision—if any one asked what was the actual
nature of this regulator and on what foundation
it built its judgments, then were both the regulator which dwelt in the breast of every man, as
well as the judgments which appeared so natural
and self evident, revealed as phenomena which
were harder to understand than any other phenomena in the world.

So we see then that since the Persian wars
Ethics, or the investigation of this mysterious regulator of human action—the moral law—comes
to the front in Greek Philosophy. Up to this
time Greek Philosophy had been in the main natural philosophy. It made it its duty to investigate and explain the laws which hold in the world

of nature. Now nature lost interest with the philosophers ever more and more. Man, or the ethical nature of humanity, became the central point of their investigations. Natural Philosophy ceased to make further progress, the natural sciences were divided from philosophy; all progress of the ancient philosophy came now from the study of the spiritual nature of man and his morality.

The Sophists already had begun to despise the knowledge of nature. Still farther went Socrates, who was of opinion that he could learn nothing from the trees, but certainly from the human beings in the town. Plato looked on Natural Philosophy as play.

With that, however, the method of philosophy changed. Natural Philosophy is of necessity bound to rely on the observation of nature. On the other hand how is the moral nature of man to be recognized with more certainty than through the observation of our own personality? The senses can be mistaken, other men can deceive us. But we ourselves do not lie to ourselves, when we wish to be truthful. Thus finally that alone was recognized as certain knowledge which man produced from himself.

But not alone the subject and the method, but also the object of philosophy was different. Natural Philosophy aimed at the examination of the necessary connection of cause and effect. Its point of view was that of causality. Ethics on the other hand dealt with the will and duty of man, with ends and aims which he strives for. Thus its point of view is that of a conscious aim, teleology.

Now these new conceptions do not always reveal themselves with equal sharpness in all the various schools of thought.

There are two methods of explaining the moral law within us.

One can look for its roots in the obvious motive forces of human action, and as such appeared the pursuit of happiness or pleasure. Under the production of wares, the production of private producers externally independent of each other, happiness and pleasure and the conditions necessary thereto are also a private affair. Consequently men come to look for the foundation of the moral law in the individual need for happiness or pleasure. That is good that makes for the individual's pleasure, and increases his happiness. And evil is that which produces the contrary. How is it then possible that not everybody under all circumstances wishes only the good? That is explained by the fact that there are various kinds of pleasure and happiness. Evil arises when men choose a lower kind of pleasure or happiness in preference to a higher, or sacrifice a lasting pleasure to a momentary and fleeting one. Thus it arises from ignorance or short-sightedness. Accordingly Epicurus looked on the intellectual pleasures as higher than the physical because they last longer and give unalloyed satisfaction. He considers the pleasure of repose greater than the pleasure of action. Spiritual peace seems to him the greatest pleasure. In consequence all excess in pleasure is to be rejected; and every selfish action is bad, since respect, love and the help of my neighbors, as well as the prosperity and welfare of the community to which I belong are factors which are necessary to my own prosperity, which, however, I cannot attain if I only look out for myself without any scruples.

This view of Ethics had the advantage that it appeared quite natural and it was very easy to reconcile it with the needs of those who desired to content themselves with the knowledge which our senses give us of the knowable world as the real and to whom human existence appeared only a part of this world. On the other hands this view of ethics was bound to produce in its turn that materialist view of the world. Founding Ethics on the longing for the pleasure or happiness of the individual or on egoism and the materialist world concept conditioned and lent each other mutual support. The connection of both elements comes most completely to expression in Epicurus (341–270 B. C.) His materialist philosophy of nature is founded with a directly ethical aim.

The materialist view of nature is in his view alone in the position to free us from the fear which a foolish superstition awakes in us and to give us that peace of soul without which true happiness is impossible.

On the other hand, all those elements who were opposed to the materialism were obliged to reject his ethics, and *vice versa;* those who were not satisfied with this ethics were not satisfied with the materialism either. And this ethic of egoism, or the pursuit of the individual happiness, gave ample opportunity for attack. In the first place it did not explain how the moral law arose as a moral binding force, as a duty to do the right and not simply as advice, to prefer the more rational kind of pleasure to the less rational. And the speedy decisive moral judgment on good and bad is quite different from the balancing up between different kinds of pleasures or utilities. Also, finally, it is possible to feel a moral duty even in cases where the most generous interpretation can find no pleasure or utility from which the pursuit of this duty can be deduced. If I refuse to lie, although I by that means stir up public opinion forever against me, if I put my existence at stake, or even bring on myself the penalty of death, then there can be no talk of even the remotest pleasure or happiness which could transform the discomfort or pain of the moment into its opposite.

But what could the critics bring forward to explain this phenomenon? In fact nothing, even if according to their own view a great deal. Since they were unable to explain the moral law by natural means it became to them the surest and most unanswerable proof that man lived not only a natural life, but also outside of nature, that in him supernatural and non-natural forces work, that his spirit is something supernatural. Thus arose from this view the ethic of philosophic idealism and monotheism, the new belief in God.

This belief in God was quite different to the old polytheism; it differed from the latter not only in the number of the gods; it did not arise from the fact that these were reduced to one. Polytheism was an attempt to explain the process of Nature. Its gods were personifications of the forces of Nature; they were thus not over Nature, and not outside of Nature, but in her and formed a part of her. Natural Philosophy superseded them in the degree in which it discovered other than personal causation in the processes of nature, and developed the idea of law, of the necessary connection of cause and effect. The gods might here and there maintain a traditional existence for a time even in the philosophy, but only as a kind of superman who no longer played any active rôle. Even for Epicurus, despite his materialism, the gods were not dead, but they were changed into passive spectators.

Even the non-materialist ethical school of philosophy, such as was most completely represented by Plato (427–347 B. C.), and whose mythical side was far more clearly developed by the neoplatonists, especially by Plotinus (204–270 A. D.)—even this school did not find the gods necessary to explain nature, and dealt with them in no other way than did the materialists. Their idea of God did not spring out of the need to explain the natural world around us, but the ethical and spiritual nature of man. For that they required to assume a spiritual Being standing outside of and over nature, thus outside of time and space, a spiritual Being which formed the quintessence of all morality and who ruled the crowd who worked with their hands. And just as the former conceived themselves as noble, and the latter appeared to them common and vulgar, so did nature become mean and bad, the spirit on the other hand elevated and good. Man was unlucky enough to belong to both worlds, that of matter and of spirit. Thus he is half animal and half angel, and oscillates between good and evil. But just as God rules nature, has the moral in man the force to overcome the natural, the desires of the flesh and to triumph over them. More complete happiness is nevertheless impossible for man so long as he dwells in this vale of tears, where he is condemned to bear the burden of his own flesh. Only then when he is free from this and his spirit has returned to its original source — to God — can he enjoy unlimited happiness.

Thus it will be seen that God plays a very different rôle to what he does in the original Polytheism. This one God is no personification of an appearance of the outer nature, but the assumption for itself of an independent existence on the part of the spiritual (or intellectual) nature of man. Just as this is a unity so can the Godhead be no multiplicity. And its most complete philosophic form, the one God, has no other function than that of accounting for the moral law. To interfere in the course of the world in the manner of the ancient gods is not his business, here suffices, at least for philosophers, the assumption of the binding force in the natural law of cause and effect.

Certainly the more this view became popular and grew into the religion of the people, the more did a highest, all embracing and all ruling spirit take on again personal characteristics; the more did he take part in human affairs, and the more did the old gods smuggle themselves in. They came in as intermediators between God and man, as saints and angels. But even in this form the contempt for nature held good, as well as the view that the spiritual and especially the ethical nature of man was of supernatural origin and afforded an infallible proof of the existence of a supernatural world.

Between the two extremes Plato and Epicurus, there were many intermediary positions possible. Among these the most important was the Stoic Philosophy, founded by Zeno (B. C. 341–270). Just like the Platonic Philosophy it attacked those who sought to derive the moral law from the pleasure or egotism of the single passing individual; it recognized in him a higher power, standing over the individual, which can drive man to action, and which brings him pain and grief, nay even to death. But different to Plato they saw in the moral law nothing supernatural, only a product of nature. Virtue arises from the knowledge of nature; happiness is arrived, at when man acts in accordance with nature, that is in accordance with the universe or the universal Reason. To know nature and act in accordance with her, reasonably, which is the same as virtuously, and voluntarily to submit to her necessity, disregarding individual pleasure and pain, that is the way to happiness which the wise go. The study of nature is, however, only a means to the study of virtue. And nature itself is explained by the stoics from a moral point of view. The practical result of the Stoic ethics is not the search for happiness, but the contempt of pleasure and the good things of the world. But this contempt of the world was finally to serve the same end, that which appeared to Zeno as well as Epicurus as the highest — viz., a state of repose for the individual soul. Both systems of ethics arose out of the need for rest.

This intermediary position of the Stoic ethics between the Platonic and the Epicurean corresponded to the view of the universe which Stoicism drew up. The explanation of nature is by no means without importance to them, but nature appeared to them as a peculiar kind of monotheistic materialism which assumes a divine original force from which even the human soul springs. But this original force, the original fire, is bodily, it exists in and not outside of nature, and the soul is not immortal, even if it survives the human body. Finally it will be consumed by the original fire.

Stoicism and Platonism finally became elements of Christianity and overcame in this form

the materialist Epicureanism. This latter materialism could only prove satisfactory to a social
class which was satisfied with things as they
were, which found in them its pleasure and happiness, and had no need for another state of
affairs.

It was necessarily rejected by classes to whom
the world as it was seemed bad and full of pain
to the decaying class of the old aristocracy
as well as to the exploited classes — for whom
present and future in this world could only be
equally hopeless when the material world, that
is the world of experience, was the only one, and
no reliance was to be placed in an almighty spirit
who had it in his power to bring this world to
destruction. Finally materialism was bound to
be rejected by the whole society so soon as this
had so far degenerated that even the ruling classes
suffered under the state of affairs, so that even
these came to the opinion that no good could
come out of the existing world, but that this only
brought forth evil. To despise the world with
the Stoics, or look for a Redeemer from the
other side with the Christians, that was the only
alternative.

· A new element came in Christianity with the
invasions of the Barbarians, which substituted
for the decadent society of the Roman Empire
another in which the decrepit remains of the

Roman system of production and their views of
life combined with the youthful German society,
the latter being organized on the basis of the
mark, and a people of simple thought, content
to enjoy life; these elements combined to produce
a strange new formation.

On the one hand the Christian Church became
the bond which held the new state together:
here again the theory is apparently confirmed
that the spirit is stronger than matter, since the
intelligence of the Christian priesthood showed
itself strong enough to tame the brute force of
the German Barbarians. And this brute force,
springing as it did from the material world, appeared to the representatives of Christianity, in
addition, as the source of all evil, where it was
not ruled by spirit and held in check; on the other
hand they saw in the spirit the foundation of
all that was good.

Thus the new social situation only contributed
to strengthening the philosophic foundation of
Christianity and its system of ethics. But on
the other hand there came through this new
situation the joy in life and a feeling of self
confidence into society which had failed at the
time of the rise of Christendom. Even to the
Christian clergy — at least in the mass — the
world no longer appeared a vale of tears and
they acquired a capacity for enjoyment — a

happy Epicureanism, certainly a coarser form
and one which had nothing in common with the
ancient philosophy. Nevertheless the Christian
priesthood was obliged to hold to the Christian
ethic, no longer as the expression of their own
moral feeling, but as a means of maintaining
their rule over the people. And everything
forced them to recognize more and more the
philosophic foundation of this system of ethics,
namely the independence, nay the mastery of the
spirit, over the real world. Thus the new social
situation produced on the one hand a tendency
to a materialist system of ethics, while on the
other a series of reasons arose to strengthen the
traditional Christian ethic. Thus arose the
double morality, which became characteristic of
Christianity, the formal recognition of a system
of ethics which is only partially the expression
of our moral feeling and will, and consequently
of that which controls our action. In other
words, moral hypocrisy became a standing social
institution, which was never so widely spread as
under Christianity.

—Ethics and religion appeared now as inseparably bound together. Certainly the moral law
was the logical creator of the new God; but in
Christianity God appeared as the author of the
moral law. Without a belief in God, without religion, no morality. Every ethical question be-

came a theological one, and as the most original and simple form of social indignation is the moral, the feeling of moral indignation, the feeling of the immorality of the existing social institutions—so did every social uprising commence in the form of a theological criticism, to which certainly came as an additional factor the circumstance that the Church was the foremost means of class rule and the Roman Priesthood the worst exploiters in the middle ages, so that all rebellion against any form of exploitation always affected the Church in the first place.

Even after the Renaissance at a time when philosophic thought had again arisen, questions of ethics remained for a long time questions of theology.

CHAPTER II

THE ETHICAL SYSTEMS OF THE PERIOD OF THE ENLIGHTENMENT

After the Renaissance the study of nature again began to arouse interest, and with it also philosophy, which from then till well into the eighteenth century became principally natural philosophy, and as such raised our knowledge of the world to far above the level reached in the ancient world. They set out from the progress which the Arabs had made in natural science during the middle ages over the Greeks. The high-water mark of this development is certainly formed by the theory of Spinoza (1632–1677).

Ethics took a second place with these thinkers. It was subordinated to natural science, of which it formed a part. But it came again to the fore so soon as the rapid development of Capitalism in west Europe in the eighteenth century had created a similar situation to that which had been created by the economic awakening which followed on the Persian wars in Greece. Then began, to speak in modern language, a revaluing of all values, and therewith a zealous thinking out and investigation into the foundation and essence of all morality. With that went certainly an eager research into the nature of the new method of production. Simultaneously with the appearance of ethics there began a new science of which the ancients were ignorant, the special child of the capitalist system of production, whose explanation it serves: political economy.

In Ethics, however, we find three schools of thought side by side, which often run parallel to the three systems of the ancients, the Platonic, the Epicurean, and the Stoic: An anti-material-ist — the traditional Christian — a materialist, and finally a middle system between the two. The optimism and joy of life in the rising Bour-geoisie, at least in their progressive elements, especially their intellectuals, felt itself strong enough to show itself openly and to throw aside all hypocritical masks, which the ruling Chris-tianity had hitherto forced on them. And mis-erable as frequently the present might be, yet the uprising Bourgeoisie felt that the best part of reality, the future, belonged to them, and they felt the ability in themselves to change the vale of tears into a Paradise, in which man could fol-low his inclinations. In reality and in the natural impulses of man their thinkers saw the germs of all good and not all evil. This new school of thought found a thankful public not only among the more progressive elements in the Bourgeoisie, but also in the court nobility, who at that period had acquired such an absolute power in the state that even they thought that they could dispense with all Christian hypocrisy in their life of pleasure, all the more as they were now divided by a deep chasm from the life of the people. They looked on citizens and peasants as being of a lower order to whom their philosophy was incomprehensible, so that they could freely and undisturbedly develop it without fear of shaking their own means of rule, the Christian religion, and Ethics.

The conditions of the new view of life and ethics developed most vigorously in France. There they came most clearly and courageously to expression. But as in the case of the ancient Epicureanism so in the enlightenment philosophy of Lametric (1709–1751), Holbach (1723–1789), Helvetius (1715–1771), the ethic of egoism, of utility or pleasure, stood in close logical connection with a materialist view of the universe. The world as experience presents it to us appeared the only one which can be taken into account by us. The causes of this new Epicureanism had great similarity to the ancient, as well as the results at which both arrived. Nevertheless they were in one very essential point of a totally different character. The old Epicureanism did not arise as the disturber of the traditional religious views: it had understood how to accommodate itself to them. It was, however, not the theory of a revolutionary class, it did not preach war, but contemplative enjoyments. Far more was the Platonic idealism and theism the theory of the overthrow of the traditional religious views, a theory of the discontented classes.

Otherwise was it with the Philosophy of Enlightenment. Certainly even this had a conservative root, it regarded contemplative enjoyment as happiness, that is so far as it served the needs of the court nobility, which drew its living from the existing autocratic regime. But in the main it was the philosophy of the most intelligent and farthest developed as well as the most courageous elements in the Bourgeoisie. It gave them a revolutionary character. Standing from the very beginning in the most absolute opposition to the traditional religion and ethics they acquired more and more, the more the Bourgeoisie increased in strength and class consciousness, the conception of a fight — a conception which was quite strange to the old Epicureans — the fight against priests and tyrants; the fight for new ideals.

The nature and method of the moral views and the height of the moral passions are according to the French materialists determined by the

conditions of human life, especially by the constitution of the state as well as by education.
It is always self interest that determines men;
it can, however, become a very social interest, if
society is so organized that the individual interest
coincides with the interest of the community, so
that the passions of men serve the common welfare. True virtue consists in the care for the
common weal, it can only flourish where the
commonwealth at the same time advances the
interests of the individual, where he cannot damage the commonwealth without damaging himself.

It is incapacity to perceive the more durable
interests of mankind, ignorance as to the best
form of government, society and education which
renders a state of affairs possible which of necessity brings the individual interest into conflict
with that of the community. It only remains to
make an end of this ignorance, to find a form of
state, society and education corresponding to the
demands of reason, in order to establish happiness and virtue on a firm and eternal foundation.
Here we come on the revolutionary essence of
the French materialism, which indicts the existing state as the cause of immorality. With that
it raises itself above the level of Epicureanism,
with that, however, it weakens the position of
its own Ethics.

Because it is no mere question of inventing the best form of state and society; these have got to be fought for, the powers that be must be confronted and overthrown in order to establish an empire of virtue. That requires, however, great moral zeal, and where is that to come from if the existing society is so bad that it prevents altogether the growth of virtue or morality? Must not morality be already there in order that the higher society may arise? Is it not necessary that the moral should be alive in us before the moral order can become a fact? Whence, however, is a moral ideal to be derived from in a world of vice?

To that we obtain no satisfactory answer.

In very different fashion to the French did the Englishmen of the eighteenth century endeavor to explain the moral law. They showed themselves in general less bold and more inclined to compromise, in keeping with the history of England since the Reformation. Their insular position was especially favorable to their economic development during this period. They were driven thereby to make sea voyages which in the seventeenth and eighteenth centuries, thanks to the colonial system, formed the quickest road to a fortune. It kept England free from all the burdens and the ravages of wars on land, such as exhausted the European powers. Thus England acquired in the seventeenth and eighteenth centuries more wealth than all the other nations of Europe and placed herself, so far as her economic position was concerned, at their head. But when new classes and new class antagonisms and with that new social problems, arise in a country at an earlier date than elsewhere, the new classes only attain a small degree of class consciousness, and still remain to a large degree imprisoned in the old methods of thought, so that the class antagonisms only appear in a very undeveloped form. Thus in such a land it does not at once come to a final and decisive struggle in the class war, it comes to no decisive overthrow of the old classes, who there continue to rule without any limit and in all the neighboring countries remain at the height of their power. The new classes are still incapable of taking on the governments because they do not realize their own position in society, are frightened by the novelty of their own endeavors, and themselves seek for support and points of contact in the traditional relations.

So that it seems to be a general law of social development, that countries which are pioneers in the economic development are tempted to put compromise in the place of radical solutions.

Thus France stood by the side of Italy in the Middle Ages at the head of the economic devel-

opment of Europe. She came more and more
into opposition with the Papacy — their government first rebelled against Rome. But just because she opened the way in this direction, she
never succeeded in founding a national church,
and only was able to force the Papacy to a compromise which has lasted, with unimportant interruptions, up to the present. On the other
hand the most radical champions against the
Papal might were two states which were economically the most backward, Scotland and Sweden.

Since the Reformation England, together with
Scotland, has taken the place of France and Italy
as the pioneer of economic development, and
thus compromise has become for both England
and Scotland the form of the solution of
their class struggles. Just because in England, in the seventeenth century, capital acquired
power more rapidly than elsewhere, because
there earlier than in other countries, it came to a
struggle with the feudal aristocracy, did this
fight end with a compromise, and that explains
the fact that the feudal system of landed property even today is stronger in England than in
any other country of Europe—Austro-Hungary
perhaps alone excepted. For the same reason,
that of her rapid economic development, the
class war between Proletariat and Bourgeoisie
first blazed up in England of all countries in the

world. It blazed up at a time when Proletariat and industrial capitalist had not yet got over the small bourgeois methods of thought, when many and even clear-sighted observers mixed up the two classes together as the industrial class; when the type of the proletariat, self-conscious and confident in the future of his own class, as well as that of the autocrat and unlimited ruler in the state—the industrial capitalist—had not yet developed. Thus the struggle of the two classes landed, after a short and showy flare-up in a compromise which made the rule of the Bourgeoisie for many years to come more unlimited than in any other land with the modern system of production.

Naturally can the effects of this law, just as that of any other, be disturbed by unfavorable by-currents, and advanced by favorable. But in any case it was so far efficacious that it is necessary to be on our guard against the popular interpretation of the historical materialism which holds that the land which takes the lead in the economic development invariably also brings the corresponding forms of the class war to the sharpest and most decisive expression.

Even materialism and atheism as well as ethics were subject in England to the spirit of compromise, which has ruled since the sixteenth century. The fight of the democratic and rising class against the governing power, independent of the Bourgeoisie and subject to the feudal aristocracy with their court nobility and their state church, commenced in England more than a century before France, at a time when only few had got over the Christian thought. If in France the fight against the state church became a fight between Christianity and atheistic materialism, in England it became only a struggle between special democratic Christian sects and the state-church-organized sect. And if in France in the period of the enlightenment, the majority of the intelligence and the classes that came under its influence thought as materialists and atheists, so did the English intelligence look for a compromise between materialism and Christianity. Certainly materialism found its first public form in England in the theory of Thomas Hobbes (1588-1679); certainly were to be found in England thinkers on Ethical questions, whose courage surpassed that of the most courageous Frenchman, such as Mandeville (1670-1733) who declared morality to be a means of ruling, a discovery to keep the workers in subjection, and who looked on vice as the root of all social good. But such ideas had little influence on the thoughts of the many. A Christian profession remained the sign of respectability, and even if this were not felt, still to pretend to feel it became the duty of every man of learning, who did not wish to come into conflict with society.

Thus the Englishmen remained very sceptical of the materialistic ethics, which wished to found the moral law on self love, or on the pleasure and the ability of the individual. Certainly the intellectual circles of the rising Bourgeoisie sought even in England to explain the moral law as a natural phenomenon, but they saw that its compulsory might could not be explained from simple considerations of utility, and that the constructions were too artificial which were required to unite the commands of morality with the motives of utility — let alone to think of making out of the latter an energetic motive force of the former. Thus they distinguished very nicely between the sympathetic and the egoistic interests in man, recognized a moral sense which drives man to be active for the happiness of his fellows. After the Scotchman, Hutcheson (1694–1747), the most distinguished representative of this theory was Adam Smith, the economist (1723–1790). In his two principal works he investigated the two mainsprings of human action. In the "Theory of Moral Sentiments" (1759) he started out from sympathy as the most important bond of human society; his "Wealth of Nations" assumes the egoism, the material interest of the individual, to be the mainspring of human action. That book appeared in 1776, but the principles which it contained Adam Smith uttered orally in Glasgow as early as 1752 or 1753. His theory of egoism and his theory of sympathy were not mutually exclusive, but were complementary the one of the other.

If these Englishmen set egoism and moral sense over against each other, so was that, as compared to the materialists, an approach to Platonism and Christianity. Nevertheless their views were widely different from the latter. Since, while according to Christianity, man is bad by nature; and according to the Platonic theory our natural impulses are the source of evil in us, so for the English school of the eighteenth century, the moral sense was opposed certainly to egoism, but was just as much as the latter a natural impulse. Even the egoism appeared to them not as a bad, but as a fully justifiable impulse which was as necessary for the welfare of society as sympathy with others. The moral sense was a sense just as any other human sense, and in a certain degree their sixth sense.

Certainly with this assumption, just as in the case of the French materialists, the difficulty was only postponed and not solved. To the question, whence comes this peculiar sense in man, the Englishman had no answer. It was given by nature to man. That might suffice for those who traded in a creator of the universe, but it did not make this assumption superfluous.

The task for the further scientific development of ethics appeared in this state of the question clear. The French, as well as the English, school had achieved much for the psychological and historical explanation of the moral feelings and views. But neither the one nor the other could succeed in making quite clear that morality was an outcome of causes which lie in the realm of experience. The English school must be surpassed and the causes of the moral sense investigated. It was necessary to go beyond the French school and to lay bare the causes of the moral ideal.

But the development goes in no straight line. It moves in contradictions. The next step of philosophy in regard to ethics took the opposite direction. Instead of investigating the ethical nature of man in order to bring this more than ever under the general laws of nature, it came to quite other conclusions.

This step was achieved by German philosophy with Kant (1724–1804). Certain people like to cry now, " Back to Kant!" But those who mean by that the Kantian ethic, might just as well cry " Back to Plato!"

CHAPTER III

THE ETHIC OF KANT

I. THE CRITICISM OF KNOWLEDGE

Kant took the same ground as the material-ists. He recognized that the world outside of us is real and that the starting point of all knowledge is the experience of the senses. But the knowledge which we acquire from experience is partly composed of that which we acquire through the sense impressions and partly from that which our own intellectual powers supply from themselves; in other words, our knowledge of the world is conditioned not simply by the nature of the external world, but also by that of our organs of knowledge. For a knowledge of the world therefore the investigation of our own intellectual powers is equally as necessary as that of the external world. The investigation of the first is, however, the duty of philosophy — this is the science of science.

In this there is nothing contained that every materialist could not subscribe to, or that, per-haps with the exception of the last sentence had

not also been previously said by materialists.
But certainly only in the way in which certain
sentences from the materialist conception of history had already been uttered before Marx, as
conceptions which had not borne fruit. It was
Kant who first made them the foundation of his
entire theory. Through him did philosophy first
become the science of science, whose duty it is
not to teach a distinct philosophy, but how to
philosophize, the process of knowing, method-
ical thinking, and that by way of a critique of
knowledge.

But Kant went farther than this, and his great
philosophical achievement, the investigation of
the faculties of knowledge, became itself his
philosophical stumbling block.

Since our sensual experience does not reveal
to us the world as it is in itself, but only as it
is for us, as it appears to us, thanks to the peculiar constitution of our faculties of knowledge,
so the world as it is in itself must be different
to that which appears to us. Consequently Kant
distinguishes between the world of phenomena,
of appearances, and the world of things in themselves, the "noumena," or the intelligible world.
Certainly this latter is for us unknowable, it
lies outside of our experience, so that there is
no need to deal with it; one might simply take it
as a method of designating the fact that our

knowledge of the world is always limited by the nature of our intellectual faculties, is always relative, that for us there can only be relative and no absolute truths, not a final and complete knowledge, but an endless process of knowing.

But Kant was not content with that. He felt an unquenchable longing to get a glimpse into that unknown and inexplorable world of things in themselves, in order to acquire at least a notion of it.

And indeed he got so far as to say quite distinct things about it. The way to this he saw in the critique of our powers of thought.

These latter by separating from experience that which comes from the senses must arrive at the point of describing the forms of knowledge and perception as they originally and *a priori,* previous to all experience, are contained in our " feelings." In this manner he discovered the ideality of time and space. According to him these are not conceptions which are won from experience, but simply the forms of our conception of the world, which are embedded in our faculties of knowledge. Only under the form of conceptions in time and space can we recognize the world. But outside of our faculties of knowledge there is no space and no time. Thus Kant got so far as to say about the world of things in themselves, that completely unknowable world, something very distinct, namely, that it is timeless and spaceless.

Without doubt this logical development is one of the most daring achievements of the human mind. That does not say by any means that it is not open to criticism. On the contrary there is a great deal to be said against it, and in fact there are very very weighty objections which have been brought against it. The assumption of the ideality of space and time in the Kantian sense led to inextricable contradictions.

There can certainly be no doubt that our concepions of time and space are conditioned by the constitution of our faculties of knowledge, but I should have thought that that would only necessarily amount to saying, that only those connections of events in the universe can be recognized which are of such a nature as to call forth in our intellectual faculties the concepts of space and time. The ideality of time and space would then imply just as the thing in itself, no more and no less than a limit to our powers of knowing.

Relations of a kind which cannot take the form of space or time concepts — even if such really exist, that we do not know — are for us inconceivable, just as much as the ultra-violet and ultra-red rays are imperceptible for our powers of vision.

But Kant did not mean the matter in this sense
at all. Because space and time provide the forms
in which alone my faculties of knowledge can
recognize the world, he takes for granted that
time and space are forms which are only to be
found in my faculty of knowledge, and correspond to no sort of connection in the real world.
In his " Prolegomena to every future Meta-
physic " Kant compares in one place the concept of space with the concept of color. This
comparison appears to us very apt, it by no
means, however, proves what Kant wants to
prove. If cinnabar appears red to me, that fact
is certainly conditioned by the peculiarity of my
visual organs. Out of that there is no color.
What appears to me as color is called forth by
waves of æther of a distinct length which affect
my eye. Should any one wish to consider these
waves in relation to the color as the thing in itself,
which in reality they are not, then our power of
vision would not be a power to see the things
as they are, but power to see them as they are
not; not a capacity of knowledge, but of illusion.

But it is quite another matter when we look
not at one color alone, but take several colors
together and distinguish them from one another.
Each of them is called forth by distinct ether
waves of different lengths. To the distinctions
in the colors there correspond differences in the

lengths of the ether waves. These distinctions
do not lie in my organ of vision but have their
ground in the external world. My organs of
vision have only the function of making me conscious of this difference in a certain form, that
of color. As a means to a recognition of this distinction it is a power of real knowledge and not
of illusion. These distinctions are no mere appearances. That I see green, red and white, that
has its ground in my organ of sight. But that
the green is different to the red, that testifies
to something that lies outside of me, to a real
difference between the things.

Besides that the peculiarity of my organ has
the effect that by its means I can only recognize
the motions of the ether. No other communication from the outer world can reach me through
that medium.

Just as with the power of vision in particular
so is it with the organs of knowledge in general.
They can only convey to me Space and Time
conceptions, that is, they can only show me those
relations of the things which can call forth Time
and Space conceptions in my head. To impressions of another kind, if there are any, they
cannot react. And my faculty of knowledge renders it possible for me to obtain these impressions
in a particular way. So far are the categories of

space and time founded in the construction of my faculty of knowledge.

But the relations and distinctions of the things themselves, which are shown to me by means of the individual space and time concepts, so that the different things appear to me as big and small, near and far, sooner or later, are real relations and distinctions of the external world, which are not conditioned through the nature of my faculty of knowledge.

Even if we therefore are not in a position to recognize a single thing by itself, if our faculty of knowledge is in respect to that a faculty of ignorance, we can yet recognize the real differences between things. These distinctions are no mere appearances, even if our conception of them is conveyed to us by means of appearances; they exist outside of us, and can be recognized by us, certainly only in certain forms.

Kant, on the other hand, was of the opinion that not simply are space and time forms of conception for us, but that even the temporal and spacial differences of phenomena spring solely from our heads, and indicate nothing real. If that were really so, then would all phenomena spring simply from our heads, since they all take the form of temporal and spacial differences. Thus we could know absolutely nothing about the world outside of us, not even that it existed.

Should there exist a world outside of us, then, thanks to the ideality of space and time, our faculty of knowledge would be not an imperfect, one-sided mechanism, which communicated to us only a one-sided knowledge of the world, but a complete mechanism of its kind, and one which served to completely cut us off from all knowledge of the world. Certainly a mechanism to which the name "Faculty of Knowledge" is just about as suitable as the fist to the eye.

Kant could attack ever so energetically the "mystical" idealism of Berkeley, which he hoped to replace with his critical idealism. His criticism took a turn, which nullifies his own assumption that the world is real and only to be known through experience, and thus mysticism cast out from the one side finds on the other a wide triumphal doorway open, through which it can enter with a flourish of trumpets.

II. THE MORAL LAW

Kant assumed as his starting point that the world is really external to us and does not simply exist in our heads, and that knowledge about it is only to be attained through experience. His philosophical achievement was to be the examination of the conditions of experience, of the boundaries of our knowledge. But just this very examination became for him an incitement to surmount this barrier, and to discover an unknowable world, of which he actually knew that it was of quite another nature than the world of appearances, that it was completely timeless and spaceless, and therefore causeless as well.

But why this break-neck leap over the boundaries of knowledge which caused him to lose all firm ground under the feet? The ground could not be a logical one, since through this leap he landed in contradictions which nullified his own assumptions. It was a historical ground which awaked in him the need for the assumption of a supersensuous world — a need which he must satisfy at all price.

If, in the eighteenth century, France was a hundred years behind England, just so much was Germany behind France. If the English bourgeoisie no longer needed the materialism, since without it, and on religious grounds, they had got rid of the feudalist state and its church, the German bourgeoisie did not yet feel strong enough to take up openly the fight against the state and its church. They therefore withdrew in fear from the materialism. This came in the eighteenth century to Germany, just as to Russia, not as the philosophy of conflict but of pleasure, in a form suitable to the needs of the "enlightened" despotism. It grew at the princely courts, side by side with the narrowest orthodoxy. In the bourgeoisie there remained, however, even in its boldest and most independent pioneers, as a rule, some relic of Christian belief, from which they could not emancipate themselves.

That was bound to make the English philosophy appeal to German philosophers. In fact they had also a very great influence on Kant. I cannot remember ever to have found in his writings any mention of a French materialist of the eighteenth century. On the other hand he quoted with preference Englishmen of the seventeenth and eighteenth centuries, Locke, Hume, Berkeley and Priestley.

But between the German and English philosophy there was a great difference. The English philosophized at a time of great practical advance, of great practical struggles.

The practice captured their entire intellectual force; even their philosophy was entirely ruled by practical considerations. Their philosophers were greater in their achievements in economics, politics, natural science, than in philosophy.

The German thinkers found no practice which could prevent them from concentrating their entire mental power on the deepest and most abstract problems of science. They were therefore in this respect without their like outside of Germany. That was not founded on any race quality of the Germans, but on the circumstances of the time. In the sixteenth and seventeenth centuries the deepest philosophic thinkers were to be found in Italy, France, Holland, England, and not in Germany. The quiet that came over German political life in the century following the Thirty Years War first gave Germany the lead in Philosophy, just as Marx's " Capital " had its origin in the period of reaction following on 1848.

Kant, despite his sympathy for the English, could not find satisfaction in their philosophy. He was just as critical towards it as towards materialism.

In both cases Ethics was bound to strike him as the weakest point. It seemed to him quite impossible to bring the moral law into a necessary connection with nature ; that is, with the world of phenomena. Its explanation required another world, a timeless and spaceless world of pure spirit, a world of freedom in contrast to the world of appearances (phenomena) which is ruled by the necessary chain of cause and effect. On the other hand his Christian feelings, the outcome of a pious education, were bound to awaken the need for the recognition of a world in which God and immortality were possible.[1]

[1]As a curiosity it may be mentioned here that it is possible to confront Bernstein's witty remark "Kant against Cant" with the fact that Kant himself was Cant. "His ancestors came from Scotland. . . . The father, a saddler by profession, maintained in his name the

As Kant had to allow that God and immortality were completely superfluous in the world of
our experience, he was obliged to look for a
world "beyond" experience for them, and thus
the spaceless and timeless world of things in
themselves corresponded most completely to his
needs.

Kant obtained the best proof for the existence
of God and immortality in this world of the
"beyond" from the moral laws. Thus we find
with him, as with Plato, that the repudiation of
the materialist explanation and the belief in a
special world of spirits, or if it is preferred a
world of spirit, lend each other mutual support
and render it necessary.

How, however, did Kant manage to obtain
farther insight into this spirit world? The critique
of pure reason only allowed him to say of it,
that it was timeless and spaceless. Now this
spacelessness has to be filled up with a content.
Even for that Kant has an idea.

Scottish spelling Cant, the Philosopher first changed the
letters to prevent the false pronunciation as Zant.
[Kuno Fischer History of Modern Philosophy, Vol. III.,
p. 52, German Ed.] His family was very religious
and this influence Kant never got over. Not less than
Kant is the "cant" related to puritan piety. The word
signifies first the puritan method of singing, then the
puritan religious and finally the customary, thoughtless
oft-repeated phraseology to which men submit themselves. Bernstein appealed, in his "Assumptions of Socialism," for a Kant as an ally against the materialist
"party-cant."

The unknowable world of things in themselves becomes at least partly knowable directly one succeeds in getting hold of a thing in itself. And Kant finds this for us. *It is the personality of man.* I am for myself at once phenomenon and thing in itself. My pure reason is a thing in itself. As a part of the sensuous world I am subject to the chain of cause and effect, therefore to necessity; as a thing in itself I am free, that is, my actions are not determined by the causes of the world of the senses, but by the moral law dwelling within me, which springs from the pure reason and calls out to me not " Thou must," but " Thou shalt." This shall were an absurdity if there did not correspond to it, a can, if I were not free.

The moral freedom of man is certainly a complicated thing. It brings along with it certainly no less contradictions than the ideality of time and space. Since this freedom comes to expression in actions which belong to the world of phenomena, but as such fall into the chain of cause and effect,—they are necessary. The same actions are at the same time free and necessary. Besides this freedom arises in the timeless, intelligible world, while cause and effect always fall in a particular time. The same time-determined action has thus a time, as well as a cause in time.

But what is now the moral law, which from the world of things in themselves, the "world of the understanding, extends its working right into the world of appearances, the world of the "senses," and then subordinates itself? Since it springs from the world of the understanding its determining ground can only lie in the pure reason. It must be of a purely formal nature, because it must remain fully free from all relation to the world of the senses, which would at once involve a relation of cause and effect, a determining ground of the will which would at once annihilate its freedom.

"There is, however," says Kant in his Critique of Practical Reason, "besides the matter of the law, nothing further contained than the law-giving form. Thus the law-giving form, so far as it is contained in the maxim, is the only thing that can constitute a determining ground of the free will."

From that he draws the following "Fundamental Law of the Pure Practical Reason."

"Act so that the maxim of thy action may be a principle of universal legislation."

This principle is by no means startlingly new. It forms only the philosophic translation of the ancient precept, to do unto others as we would be done by. The only new thing is the declaration that this precept forms a revelation of an intelligible world; a revelation which with the greatest application of philosophic insight was to be discovered as a principle which applied not only for humanity, "but for all finite Beings who possess Reason and will, nay even including the Infinite Being as the highest intelligence."

Unfortunately the proof for this law which applies even to the Supreme Intelligence shows a very serious flaw. It ought to be "independent of all conditions appertaining to the world of the senses," but that is easier said than fulfilled. Just as little as it is possible with the air pump to create a completely airless space; just as it must always contain air, though it be in so refined degree, that it is no more to be recognized by us, in the same way we cannot possibly grasp a thought, which is independent of all conditions appertaining to the world of the senses. Even the moral law does not escape this fate.

The moral law already includes conditions which belong to the world of the senses. It is not a law of the "pure will" in itself, but a law of the control of my will when brought in contact with my fellow men. It assumes this; for me, however, these appearances are from the world of the senses.

And still more is assumed, however, by the conception of the moral law: "act so that the maxim of thy action may be a principle of universal legislation." This assumes not only men outside of me, but also the wish that these fellow men should behave themselves in a particular manner. They are so to behave themselves as the moral law prescribes to me to act. Not only society but also a distinct form of social conditions is assumed as possible and desirable.

That in fact the need for such is concealed in the ground of his "practical reason" and determines his spaceless and timeless moral law, Kant himself betrays in his "Critique of Practical Reason" in a polemic against the deduction of the moral law from pleasure.[1]

It is therefore surprising that intelligent men could have thought of calling the desire for happiness a universal *practical law,* on the ground that the desire is universal and therefore also the *maxim* by which everyone makes this desire determine his will.

"For, whereas, in other cases a universal law of nature makes everything harmonious, here, on the contrary, if we attribute to the maxim the universality of law the extreme opposite of harmony will follow, the greatest opposition and the complete distraction of the maxim itself and its purpose. For, in that case, the will of all has not one and the same object, but everyone has his

[1] Kant's "Critique of Practical Reason," Tr. by T. W. Abbott. Lond. 1889. Sect. 10, theorem II, pp. 115-6.

own (his private welfare), which may accidentally accord with the purposes of others which are equally selfish, but it is far from sufficiency for a law, because the occasional exceptions which one is permitted to make are endless and cannot be definitely embraced in a universal rule. In this manner there results a harmony like a married couple bent on going to ruin. "O, marvellous harmony, what he wishes, she wished also," or like what is said of the pledge of Francis I, to the Emperor Charles V.: "What my brother Charles wishes, that I wish also" (viz. Milan).

Thus pleasure is not to be a maxim which can serve as a principle of universal legislation, and that because it can call forth social disharmonies. The moral law has thus to create a harmonious society, and such must be possible, otherwise it would be absurd to wish to create it. The Kantian moral law assumes thus, in the first place, a harmonious society as desirable and as possible. But it also assumes that the moral law is the means to create such a society, that this result can be achieved through a rule which the individual sets to himself. We see how thoroughly Kant was deceived, when he thought that his moral law was independent from all conditions appertaining to the world of sense, and that it formed thus a principle which would apply to all timeless and spaceless spirits, including God Almighty himself.

In reality Kant's moral law is the result of very concrete social needs. Naturally, since it springs from the wish for a harmonious society, it is possible to deduce from it the ideal of a harmonious society and thus it has been possible to stamp Kant as a founder of Socialism. Cohen repeats this again also in his latest work " Ethics of the Pure Will " (Ethik des reinen Willens) 1905. In reality, however, Kant is far farther removed from Socialism than the French materialism of the eighteenth century. While according to these the Moral Law was determined by the condition of the state and society, so that the reform of morality rendered in the first place necessary the reform of the State and Society, and so the fight against immorality widened itself into a fight against the ruling powers; according to Kant the society which exists in time and space is determined by a moral law standing outside of time and space, which directs its commands to the individual not the society. Is the morality of the individual imperfect, one must not lay the blame for that on the State and Society, but in the fact that man is not entirely angel, but half animal and consequently always being drawn down by his animal nature, against which he can only fight through the raising and the purifying of his own inner man. The individual must improve himself if the Society is to be improved.

It is clear that Socialism takes peculiar forms if we look on Kant as its founder. This peculiarity will be in no way diminished when we observe the farther development of the moral law by him. From the moral law springs the consciousness of Personality, and the dignity of man, and the phrase: " Act so, that you, as well in your own person as in the person of every other, at all times look on man as end, and never simply as a means."

" In those words," says Cohen (pp. 303-4) " is the deepest and most far-reaching sense of the categoric imperative brought to expression; they contain the moral programme of the new time and the *entire future world history*. The idea of the final (or end) advantage of Humanity becomes thereby transformed into the idea of Socialism, by which every man is defined as a final end, as an end in itself."

The programme of the " entire future world history " is conceived in somewhat narrow fashion. The " timeless moral law, that man ought to be an end, and at no time simply a means, has itself only an " end " in a society in which men are used by other men simply as means to their ends. In a communist society, this possibility disappears and with that goes the necessity of the Kantian Programme for the " entire future world history." What becomes then of this? We have then in the future either no Socialism, or no world history to expect.

The Kantian Moral Law was a protest against the very concrete feudal society with its personal relations of dependency. The would-be " socialist " principle which fixes the Personality and Worth of men is accordingly just as consistent with Liberalism or Anarchism as with Socialism, and contains, in no greater degree any new idea than the one already quoted, of the universal legislation. It amounts to the philosophical formula for the idea of " Freedom, Equality and Fraternity " already then developed by Rousseau, and which, moreover, was to be found in primitive Christianity. The only thing Kantian, even here, is simply the mere form in which this principle is proved.

The dignity of Personality is namely derived from the fact, that it is a part of a super-sensuous world, that as a moral being it stands outside nature and over nature. Personality is " Freedom and Independence from the mechanism of the entire nature," so that " the person as belonging to the world of sense is subordinate to its own personality, so far as it belongs to the world of intelligence." Thus it is not then to be wondered if man, as belonging to both worlds, is obliged to look on his own being with regard to its second and highest qualification, not otherwise than with respect and to conceive the greatest respect for the laws of the same.   With that we would be happily arrived again at the primitive Christian argument for the equality of all men, which necessarily arises from the fact that we are all children of God.

III. FREEDOM AND NECESSITY

Meanwhile, reject as we must the assumption of the two worlds to which, according to Plato and Kant, man belongs, it is nevertheless true that man lives at the same time in two worlds, and the moral law inhabits one of them, which is not the world of experience.   But all the same even this world is no super-sensuous one.   The two worlds, in which man lives, are the Past and the Future. The Present forms the boundary of the two.   His whole experience lies in the past, all experience is past, and all the connecting links which past experience shows him lie with inevitable necessity before, or still more, behind him.   In these there is nothing more left to alter, he can do nothing more in regard to them than recognize their necessity.   Thus is the world of experience the world of knowing, and the world of necessity.

It is otherwise with the Future.   Of it I have

not the smallest experience. Apparently free it lies before me, as the world which I do not explore as one knowing it, but in which I have to assert myself as an active agent. Certainly I can extend the experience of the past into the future, certainly I can conclude that these will be even so necessarily determined as those, but even if I can only recognize the world on the assumption of necessity, yet I shall only be able to act in it on the assumption of a certain Freedom. Even if compulsion is exercised over my actions, there remains to me the choice, whether I shall yield to it, or not, there remains to me as last resort the possibility of withdrawing myself by a voluntary death. Action implies continual choice between various possibilities, and be it alone that of doing or not doing, it means accepting or rejecting, it means defending and opposing. Choice, however, assumes in advance the possibility of choice just as much as the distinction between the acceptable and the inacceptable, the good and the bad. The moral judgment, which is an absurdity in the world of the past, the world of experience, in which there is nothing to choose, where iron necessity rules, is unavoidable in the world of the unknown future — of freedom.

⌂ But not simply the feeling of freedom is assumed by action, but also certain aims. If in the world of the past, the sequence of cause and effect (causality) rules, so in the world of action, of the future; the thought of aim (Teleology). For action the feeling of freedom is an indispensable psychological necessity, which is not to be got rid of by any degree of knowledge. Even the sternest Fatalism, even the deepest conviction that man is a necessary product of his circumstances, cannot bring it about that we cease to love, and to hate, to defend and attack.

But all that is no monopoly of man but holds also of the animals. Even these have freedom of the will, in the sense that man has, namely as a subjective, inevitable feeling of freedom, which springs from ignorance of the future and the necessity of exercising a direct influence on it.

And just in the same way they have command of a certain insight into the connection of cause and effect. Finally the conception of an end is not quite strange to them. In respect of insight into the past and the necessity of nature on the one hand, and on the other in respect of the power of foreseeing the future, and the setting up of aims for their action the lowest specimens of humanity are distinguished far less from the animals than from civilized men.

The setting up of aims is not, however, anything which exists outside the sphere of necessity, of cause and effect. Even though I set up aims for myself only in the future, in the sphere of apparent freedom, yet the act of setting up aims itself, from the very moment when I set up the aim, belongs to the past, and can thus in its necessity be recognized as the result of distinct causes. That is not in any way altered by the fact that the attainment of the end is still in the future, in the sphere of uncertainty, thus in this sense in that of freedom. Let the attainment of the end be assumed as ever so far distant, the setting up of the aim itself lies in the past. In the sphere of freedom there lie only those aims which are not yet set up, of which we do not even know anything as yet.

The world of conscious aims is thus not the world of freedom in opposition to that of necessity. For each of the aims which we set ourselves, just as for each one of the means which we apply to its attainment, the causes are already given and are under certain circumstances recognizable as those which brought about the setting up of these aims and determined the way in which that was to be achieved.

It is impossible, however, to distinguish the realm of necessity and that of freedom simply as past and future; their distinction often coincides also with that of nature and society, or to be more exact, of society and that other nature from which the former displays only one particular and peculiar portion.

If we look at nature in the narrower sense, as apart from Society and then both in their relation to the future, we find at once a serious difference. The natural conditions change much slower than the Social. And the latter are at the period when men commence to philosophise, at the period of the production of wares, of a highly complicated nature, whereas there are in nature a large number of simple processes, whose subjection to law can be relatively easily perceived.

The consequence is, that despite our apparent freedom of action in the future, this action, nevertheless as far as nature is concerned comes to be looked on as determined at an early period. Dark as the future lies before me, I know of a certainty that summer will follow winter, that to-morrow the sun will rise, that to-morrow I shall have hunger and thirst, that in winter the need for warming myself will occur to me, and that my action will never be directed to escaping these natural necessities, but with the idea of satisfying them. Thus I recognize, despite all apparent freedom that in face of nature my action is necessarily conditioned. The constitution of nature external to us and of my own body produce necessities which force on me a certain willing and acting which being given according to experience can be reckoned with in advance.

It is quite otherwise with my conduct to my

fellow men, my social actions. In this case the external and internal causes, which necessarily determine my action, are not so easy to recognize. Here I meet with no overpowering forces of nature, to which I am obliged to submit myself, but with factors on a level with myself, men like myself, who by nature have no more strength than I have. Over against these I feel myself to be free, but they also appear to me to be free in their relations to their fellow men. Towards them I feel love and hate, and on them and my relations to them I make moral judgments.

The world of freedom and of the moral law is thus certainly another than that of recognized necessity, but it is no timeless and spaceless and no super-sensual world, but a particular portion of the world of sense seen from a particular point of view. It is the world as seen in its approach to us, the world on which we have to work, which we have to rearrange, before all. ‑

But what is to-day the future will be to-morrow past; thus what to-day is felt to be free action will be recognized to-morrow as necessary action. The moral law in us, which regulates this action, ceases, however, with that to appear as an uncaused cause, it falls into the sphere of experience and can be recognized as the necessary effect of a cause — and only as such cause are we at all able to recognize it, or can it become an object of

Science. In that he transferred the moral from the " this side," the sensual world, to the " other side," the super-sensual world, Kant has not advanced the scientific knowledge of it, but has closed all access to it. This obstacle must be got rid of before everything else, we must rise above Kant if we are to bring the problem of the moral law nearer to its solution.

IV. THE PHILOSOPHY OF RECONCILIATION

The Ethic forms the weakest side of the Kantian Philosophy. And all the same it is just through the Ethic that it has won its greatest success, because it met very powerful needs of the time.

The French Materialism had been a philosophy of the fight against the traditional methods of thought, and consequently against the institutions which rested on them. An irreconcilable hatred against Christianity made it the watchword, not only of the fight against the church, but of that against all the social and political forces which were bound up with it.

Kant's Critique of the Pure Reason equally drives Christianity from out of the Temple; but the discovery of the origin of the moral law, which is brought about by the Critique of the Practical Reason, opens for it again the door with all due respect. Thus through Kant, Philosophy became, instead of a weapon of the fight against the existing methods of thought and institutions, a means of reconciling the antagonisms.

But the way of development is that of struggle. The reconciliation of antagonisms implies the stoppage of development. Thus the Kantian Philosophy became a conservative factor.

The greatest advantage thereby was drawn by theology. It emancipated this from the quandary, into which the traditional belief had fallen through the development of science, in that it rendered it possible to reconcile science and religion.

" No other science," says Zeller, " experienced the influence of the Kantian Philosophy in a higher degree than the Theology. Here Kant found the soil best prepared for his principles; with that, however, he brought to the traditional methods of thought a reform and an increase in depth, which it was badly in need of. (*Geschichte der deutschen Philosophie*, 1873, p. 519.)

Just after the outbreak of the French Revolution a specially strong need arose for a theology, which was in a position to hold its own against materialism, and to drive it out of the field among educated people. Zeller writes then further.

" Kant's religious views corresponded exactly both to the moral and intellectual need of the time; it recommended itself to the enlightened, by its reasonableness, its independence of the positive, its purely practical tendency; to the religious by its moral severity and its lofty conceptions of Christianity and its founder." German theology from now on took Kant as their authority. " His Moral Theology became after a few years the foundation on which Protestant theology in Germany almost without exception, even the Catholic to a very large extent, was built up. The Kantian Philosophy, exercised for that reason, that the majority of German theologians for close on fifty years took their start from it, a highly permanent and far-reaching influence on the general education.

Vorländer quotes in his History of Philosophy (Leipzig 1903) the word of a modern German Theologian, Ritschl, who declared:

" Thus the development of the method of knowledge by Kant implied at the same time a practical rebirth of Protestantism. (Vol. II, p. 476.)"

The great Revolution created the soil for the influence of Kant, which was strongest in the two decades after the Terror. Then this influence became paler and paler. The Bourgeoisie acquired after the thirties, even in Germany, strength and courage for more decided struggles against the existing forms of State and thought, and to an absolute recognition of the world of the senses as the only real one. Thus through the Hegelian dialectic there arose new forms of Materialism, and just in the most vigorous form in Germany, for the very reason that their Bourgeoisie was well behind that of France and England; because they had not conquered the existing state machine; because they had that still to upset, therefore they required a fighting philosophy and not one of reconciliation.

In the last decades, however, their desire to fight has greatly diminished. Even though they have not attained all that they wish, yet they have all which was necessary for their development. Further struggles on a large scale, energetic fights against the existing, must be of much less use to them than to their great enemy, the proletariat, that grew in a most menacing fashion and now for its part required a fighting philosophy. This was so much the more susceptible to the influence of materialism, the more the development of the world of the senses showed the absurdity of the existing order and the necessity of its victory.

The Bourgeoisie, on the other hand, became more and more susceptible to a philosophy of reconciliation, and thus Kantism was aroused to a fresh life. This resurrection was prepared in the

reactionary period after 1848 by the then com-
mencing influence of Schopenhauer.

But in the last decade the influence of Kant has
found its way into Economics and Socialism.
Since the laws of Bourgeois Society, which were
discovered by the Classical Economists, showed
themselves more clearly as laws which made the
class war and the disappearance of the Capitalist
order necessary, the Bourgeois Economists took
refuge in the Kantian Moral Code, which being
independent of Time and Space must be in a
position to reconcile the class antagonisms and
prevent the Revolutions which take place in
Space and Time.

Side by side with the ethical school in Economics we got an ethical Socialism, when endeavors
were made in our ranks to modify the class antagonisms, and to meet at least a section of the
Bourgeoisie half way. This policy of Reconciliation also began with the cry: Back to Kant! And
with a repudiation of materialism, since it denies
the Freedom of the Will.

Despite the categoric imperative, which the
Kantian Ethic cries to the individual, its historical
and social tendency, from the very beginning on
till today, has been that of toning down, of reconciling the antagonisms, not of overcoming them
through struggle.

CHAPTER IV

The Ethic of Darwinism

I. THE STRUGGLE FOR EXISTENCE

Kant, like Plato, had divided mankind into two parts, a natural and a supernatural, an animal and an angelic. But the strong desire to bring the entire world, including our intellectual functions, under a unitary conception, and to exclude all factors besides the natural from it, or in other words the materialist method of thought, was too deeply grounded in the circumstances for Kant to be able to paralyze it for any length of time. And the splendid progress made by the natural sciences, which began just at the very time of Kant's death to make a spurt forwards, brought a series of new discoveries, which more and more filled up the gap between man and the rest of nature, and among other things revealed the fact that the apparently angelic in man was also to be seen in the animal world, and thus was of animal nature.

All the same the Materialist Ethics of the nineteenth century, so far as it was dominated by the conceptions of natural science, equally in the bold and outspoken form which it took in Germany, as well as in the more retiring and modest English, and even now French version, did not get beyond that which the eighteenth century had taught. Thus Feuerbach founded morality on the desire for happiness, Auguste Comte, the founder of Positivism, took on the other hand from the English the distinction between moral or altruistic feelings, and the egoistical, both of which are equally rooted in human nature.

A great and decided advance over this position was first made by Darwin, who proved in his book on the Descent of Man, that the altruistic feelings formed no peculiarity of man, that they are also to be found in the animal world, and that there, as here, they spring from similar causes, which are in essence identical and which have called forth and developed all the faculties of beings endowed with the power of moving themselves. With that almost the last barrier between man and animal was torn down. Darwin did not follow up his discoveries any further, and yet they belong to the greatest and most fruitful of the human intellect, and enable us to develop a new critique of knowledge.

When we study the organic world, it shows to us, in contrast to the inorganic, one very striking peculiarity: We find in it adaptation to end. All organized beings are constructed and endowed more or less with a view to an end. The end which they serve is nevertheless not one which lies outside of them. The world as a whole has no aim. The aim lies in the individuals themselves, its parts are so arranged and fitted out, that they serve the individual, the whole. Purpose and division of labor arise together. The essence of the organism is the division of labor just as much as adaptation to end. One is the condition of the other.

The division of labor distinguishes the organism from inorganic individuals, for example, crystals. Even crystals are distinct individuals with a distinct form. They grow, when they find the necessary material for their formation under the requisite conditions, but they are through and through symmetrical. On the other hand the lowest organism is a vesicle much less visible and less complicated than a crystal, but a vesicle whose external side is different, and has different functions to the inner.

That the division of labor is one which is suitable for the purpose, that is, one which is useful to the individual, renders his existence possible, or even ameliorates it, seems wonderful. But it would be still more wonderful if individuals maintained themselves and procreated with a division of labor which was not suitable for the

purpose, which rendered their existence difficult
or even impossible.

But what is the work which the organs of the
organism have to accomplish? This work is the
struggle for life, that is, not the struggle with
other organisms of the same kind, as the word is
occasionally used, but the fight with the whole of
nature. Nature is in continual movement and is
always changing her forms, hence only such individuals will be able to maintain their form for
any period of time in this eternal change who
are in a position to develop particular organs
against those external influences which threaten
the existence of the individual as well as to
supply the place of those parts which it is obliged
to give up continually to the external world.
Quickest and best will those individuals and
groups assert themselves, whose weapons of defence and instruments for obtaining food are the
best adapted to their end, that is best adapted to
the external world, to avoid its dangers and to
capture the sources of food. The uninterrupted
process of adaptation, and the selection of the
fittest, by means of the struggle for existence
produce, under such circumstances as usually
form themselves on the earth since it has bourne
organized beings, an increasing division of labor.
In fact the more developed the division of labor
is in a society, the more advanced does that so-

ciety appear to us. The continual process of rendering the organic world more perfect is thus the result of the struggle for existence in it — and that probably for a long time to come will be its future result, that is as long as the conditions of our planet do not essentially alter. Certainly we have no right to look on this process as a necessary law for all time. That would amount to imputing to the world an end which is not to be found in it.

The development need not always proceed at the same rate. From time to time periods can come, when the various organisms, each in its way, arrive at the highest possible degree of adaptation to the existing conditions, that is, are in the most complete harmony with their surroundings. So long as these conditions endure they will develop no farther, but the form which has been arrived at will develop into a fixed type, which procreates itself unchanged. A further development will only then occur when the surroundings undergo a considerable alteration, when the inorganic nature is subject to changes which disturb the balance of the organic. Such changes, however, take place from time to time, either single, sudden and violent, or numerous and unnoticed, the sum total and effect of which, however, equally brings on new situations, as for example alterations in the ocean currents, in the surface of the earth, perhaps even in the position of the planet in the universe, which bring about climatic changes, transform thick forests into deserts of sand, cover tropical landscapes with icebergs and *vice versa*. These alterations render new adaptations to the changed conditions necessary, they produce migrations which likewise bring the organisms into new surroundings, and produce fresh struggles for life between the old inhabitants and the new incomers, exterminate the badly adapted and the unadaptable individuals and types, and create new divisions of labor, new functions and new organs or transform the old. It is not always the highest developed organisms which best assert themselves by this new adaptation. Every division of labor implies a certain one-sidedness. Highly developed organs, which are specially adapted for a particular method of life, are for another far less useful than organs which are less developed, and in that particular method of life less effective, but more many-sided and more easily adaptable. Thus we see often higher developed kinds of animals and plants die out, and lower kinds take over the farther development of new higher organisms. Probably man is not sprung from the highest type of apes, the man apes, which are tending to die out, but from a lower species of four-handed animals.

II. SELF-MOVEMENT AND INTELLIGENCE

At an early period the organisms divided themselves into two great groups—those which developed the organs of self motion, and those which lacked it, animals and plants.

It is clear that the power of self movement is a mighty weapon in the struggle for life. It enables it to follow its food, to avoid danger, to bring its young into places where they will be best secured from dangers and which are best provided with food.

Self motion, however, necessarily implies an intelligence, and *vice versa.* The one of these factors without the other is absolutely useless. Only in combination do they become a weapon in the struggle for life. The power of self-movement is completely useless, when it is not combined with a power to recognize the world in which I have to move myself. What use would the legs be to the stag, if he had not the power to recognize his enemies and his food grounds? On the other hand, for a plant intelligence of any kind would be useless. Were the blade of grass able to see, hear or smell the approaching cow, that would not in the least help it to avoid being eaten.

Self-movement and intelligence thus necessarily go together, one without the other is use-

less. Wherever these faculties may spring from
they invariably come up together and develop
themselves jointly. There is no self-movement
without intelligence, and no intelligence without
self-movement. And together they serve the
same ends, the securing and alleviation of the
individual existence.

As a means to that they and their organs are
developed and perfected by the struggle for life,
but only as a means thereto. Even the most
highly developed intelligence has no capacities
which would not be of use as weapons in the
struggle for existence. Thus is explained the
one-sidedness and the peculiarity of our intelligence.

To recognize things in themselves may appear to many philosophers an important task;
for our existence it is highly indifferent, whatever we have to understand by the thing in itself.
On the other hand for every being endowed with
power of movement it is of the greatest importance to rightly distinguish the things and to
recognize their relations to one another. The
sharper his intelligence in this respect the better
service will it do him. For the existence of the
singing bird it is quite indifferent what those
things may be in themselves which appear to it
as a berry, a hawk, or a thunder cloud. But indispensable is it for his existence to distinguish

exactly berries, hawks, and clouds from the other things among his surroundings, since that alone puts him in a position to find his food, to escape the enemy, and to reach shelter in time. It is thus inevitable that the intelligence of the animal should be a power of distinguishing in space.

But just as indispensable is it to recognize the sequence of the things in time, and indeed their necessary sequence as cause and effect. Since the movement as cause can only bring as a universal result the maintenance of existence, if it aims at special more immediate or remoter effects which are so much the more easily to be achieved, the better the individual has got to learn these effects with their causes. To repeat the above example of a bird, it is not sufficient that it should know how to distinguish berries, hawks, and thunder clouds from the other things in space, it must also know that the enjoyment of the berries has the effect of satisfying its hunger, that the appearance of the hawk will have the effect that the first small bird which it can grasp will serve it as food, and that the rising thunder clouds produce storm, rain, and hail as results.

Even the lowest animal, so soon as it possesses a trace of ability to distinguish and self movement, developes a suspicion of causality. If the earth shakes, that is a sign for the worm that danger threatens and an incentive to flight.

Thus if the intelligence is to be of use to the animal in its movements it must be organized so that it is in a position to show him the distinctions in time and space as well as the causal connections.

But it must do even more. All the parts of the body serve only one individual, only one end, the maintenance of the individual. The division of labor must never go so far that the individual parts become independent, because that would lead to the dismemberment of the individual. They will work so much the more efficiently, the tighter the parts are held together, and the more uniform the word of command. From this follows the necessary unity of the consciousness. If every part of the body had its own intellectual organs, or did each of the senses which conveys to us a knowledge of the outer world produce its own consciousness, then would all knowledge of the world in such a case and the coöperation of the various members of the body be much impeded, the advantages of the division of labor would be abolished, or changed into disadvantages, the support which the senses or the organs of movement mutually give to each other would cease and there would come instead mutual hindrance.

Finally, however, the intelligence must possess in addition the power to gather experiences and

to compare. To return once more to our singing
bird, he has two ways open to him to find out
what food is the best for him and where it is
easiest to be found; what enemies are dangerous
for him and how to escape them. One, his own
experience, the other the observation of other
and older birds, who have already made experience. No master is, as is well known, born.
Every individual can so much the easier maintain
himself in the struggle for life, the greater his
experience and the better arranged they are; to
that, however, belongs the gift of memory and
the capacity to compare former impression with
later, and to extract from the common and universal element, to separate the essential from the
unessential, that is: to think. Does observation
communicate to us the differences, the particular
factor through the senses, so does thinking tell
us the common factor, the universal element in
the things.

" The universal," says Dietzgen, " is the content of all concepts, of all knowledge, of all science, of all acts of thought. Therewith the anal-
ysis of the organ of thought exhibits the latter,
as the power to investigate the universal in the
particular."

All these qualities of the intellectual powers,
we find developed in the animal world, even if
not in so high a degree as in men, and they are

often for us difficult to recognize, since it is not always easy to distinguish conscious actions springing from intelligence, from the involuntary and unconscious actions, simple reflex actions and instinctive movements which even in men play a great rôle.

If we find all these qualities of the intellectual faculties to be a necessary concomitant of the power of self movement already in the animal world, so do we, on the other hand, find in the same qualities also the same limitations which even the most embracing and most penetrating understanding of the highly developed civilized man cannot surmount.

Forces and capacities which were acquired as weapons in the battle for existence can naturally be made available for other purposes as well, besides those of rendering existence secure, when the organism has brought its power of self movement and its intelligence, as well as its instincts of which we will soon speak, to a high enough degree of development. The individual can employ the muscles, which were developed in it for the purpose of snatching its booty, or warding off the foe, as well for dancing and playing. But their particular character is obtained by these powers and capacities all the same, only from the struggle for life which developed them. Play and dance develop no particular muscles.

That holds good also of the intellectual powers
and faculties. Each was developed as a necessary
supplement to the power of self-movement in the
struggle for life, in order to render possible to the
organism the most suitable movement in the surrounding world for its own preservation, yet it
could all the same be made to serve other purposes. To these belong also pure knowing without any practical thoughts in the background,
without regard for the practical consequences
which it can bring about. But our intellectual
powers have not been developed by the struggle
for existence, to become an organ of pure knowledge, but only to be an organ which regulates our
movements in conformity with their purpose.
The more completely it functions in respect of the
latter, the more incomplete is it in the first.
From the very beginning most intimately connected with the power of self movement, it develops
itself completely only in mutual dependence on the
power of self movement and can only be brought
to perfection in this connection. Also the power
of the human faculties of cognition and human
knowledge is most intimately bound up with human practice, as we shall see.

It is the practice, however, which guarantees
to us the certainty of our knowledge.

So soon as my knowledge enables me to bring
about distinct effects, the production of which

lies in my power, the relation of cause and effect ceases for me to be simply chance or simple appearance, or simple forms of knowledge, as the pure contemplation and thought might well describe them. The knowledge of this relation becomes, through the practice, a knowledge of something real and is raised to certain knowledge.

The boundaries of practice witness certainly to the boundaries of our certain knowledge.

That theory and practice are dependent on one another and only through the mutual permeation of the one by the other can at any time the highest result attainable be arrived at, is only an outcome of the fact that movement and intellectual powers, from their earliest beginnings, were bound to go together. In the course of the development of human society the division of labor has brought it about that the natural unity of these two factors would be destroyed, and created classes to whom principally the movement, and others to whom principally the knowing, fell. We have already pointed out how this was reflected in philosophy, through the creation of two worlds, a higher or intellectual, and a lower or bodily.

But wholly were the two functions naturally in no individual to be divided, and the proletariat movement of today is directing its energies with good effect to abolishing this distinction and with it also the dualist philosophy, the philosophy of pure knowledge. Even the deepest, most abstract knowledge, which apparently is farthest removed from the practical, influence this, and are influenced by it, and to bring in us this influence to consciousness becomes the duty of a critique of human knowledge. As before, knowledge remains in the last resort always a weapon in the struggle for existence, a means to give to our movements, be they movements in nature or society, the most suitable forms and directions.

"Philosophers have only interpreted the world differently," said Marx. "The great thing, however, is to change it."

III. THE MOTIVES OF SELF MAINTENANCE AND PROPAGATION

Both powers of self movement and of knowing belong inseparably together as weapons in the struggle for existence. The one developed itself along with the other, and in the degree in which these weapons win in importance in the organism, do the other more primitive ones, which are less necessary, as for example, that of fruitfulness and of vitality diminish. On the other hand, to the degree that these diminish must the importance of the first named factors for the struggle for life increase, and it must call forth their greater development.

But self movement and knowledge form by themselves by no means a sufficient weapon in the struggle. Of what use is merely the strongest muscles, the most agile joints, the sharpest senses, the greatest understanding, in this struggle, if I do not feel in me the impulse to employ them to my preservation — if the sight of food or the knowledge of danger leaves me indifferent and awakes no emotion in me? Self movement and intellectual capacity first, then, become weapons in the struggle for existence, if with them there arises a longing for the self preservation of the organism, which brings it about that all knowledge which is of importance for its existence at once produces the will to carry out the movement necessary for its existence, and therewith calls forth this movement.

Self movement and intellectual powers are without importance for the existence of the individual without his instinct of self preservation, just as this latter again is of no importance with both the former factors. All three are most intimately bound up with each other. The instinct of self preservation is the most primitive of the animal instincts and the most indispensable. Without it no animal species endowed in any degree with the power of self movement and a faculty of intelligence could maintain itself even a short time. It rules the entire life of the animal. The same social development, which ascribes the care of the intellectual faculties to particular classes, and the practical movement to others, and produces in the first an elevation of the "spirit" over the gross "matter," goes so far in the process of isolating the intellectual faculties, that the latter, out of contempt for the "mechanical" practice which serves for the maintenance of life, comes to despise life itself. But this kind of knowledge has never as yet been able to overcome the instinct of self preservation, and to paralyze the "practise" which serves for the maintenance of life. Although many a suicide be philosophically grounded, we always, in every practical act of the denial of life, finally meet with disease or desperate social circumstances as the cause, but not a philosophical theory. Mere philosophizing cannot overcome the instinct of self preservation.

But if this is the most primitive and widely spread of all instincts it is still not the only one. It serves only for the maintenance of the individual. However long this may endure, finally it disappears without leaving any trace of its individuality behind, if it has not reproduced itself. Only those species of organisms will assert themselves in the struggle for existence, who leave a progeny behind them.

Now with the plants and the lower animals reproduction is a process which demands no power of self movement and no faculty of intelligence. That changes, however, with the animals so soon as reproduction becomes a sexual act, in which two individuals are concerned, who have to unite in order to lay either eggs and seeds (sperm) on the same spot outside of the body, or to incorporate the sperm in the body of the individual carrying the eggs. That demands a will, an impulse to find each other, to unite. Without that can the non-sexual propagation not take place, the stronger it is in the periods favorable for reproduction, so much the sooner will it take place, so much the better will be the prospects of a progeny, for the maintenance of the species. On the other hand these prospects are bad for individuals and species in whom the impulse for self reproduction is weakly developed. From a given degree of the development consequently natural selection must develop through the struggle for life an outspoken impulse to reproduction in the animal world and ever more strengthen it.

But it does not always suffice to the attainment of a numerous progeny. We have seen that in the degree in which self movement and intellectual powers grow, the number of the germs, which the individual produces, as well as its vitality, have a tendency to diminish. On the other hand

the greater the division of labor, the more complicated the organism, the longer the period which
is requisite for its development and its attainment
to maturity. Even if a part of this period is laid
in the maternal body, that has its limits. Even
from considerations of space is this body not in
a position to bear an organism as big as itself. It
must expel the young long before that period is
arrived at. From the young animals, however,
the capacities for self movement and intelligence
are the latest achieved, and they are mostly very
weakly developed as they leave the protecting
cover of the egg or the maternal body. The egg
expelled by the mother is completely without motion and intelligence. Then the care for the
progeny becomes an important function of the
mother: the hiding and defence of the eggs and
of the young, the feeding of the latter, etc. As
the impulse for reproduction, so is it with the
love for the young, especially in the animal world
is the maternal love developed as an indispensable
means, from a certain stage of the development
on, to secure the perpetuation of the species.
With the impulse towards individual self preservation these impulses have nothing to do; they
often come into conflict with it, and they can be
so strong that they overcome it. It is clear that
under otherwise equal conditions, those individuals and species have the best prospect of repro-

ducing themselves and handing on their qualities and impulses in whom the impulse of self maintenance is not able to diminish the impulse to reproduce and protect the progeny.

IV. THE SOCIAL INSTINCT

Besides these instincts which are peculiar to the higher animals, the struggle for life develops in particular kinds of animals still others, which are special and conditioned by the peculiarity of their method of life, for example, the migratory instinct, which we will not farther study. Here we are interested in another kind of instinct which is of very great importance for our subject: the social instinct.

The coöperation of similar organisms in larger crowds is a phenomenon which we can discover quite in their earliest stages: the microbes. It is explained alone by the simple fact of reproduction. If the organisms have no self movement, the progeny will consequently gather round the producer, if they are not by any chance borne away by the movements of the external world, water currents, winds, and phenomena of that sort. The apple falls, as is well known, not far from the stem, and when it is not eaten, and falls on fruitful soil, there grow from the pips young trees, which keep the old tree company.

But even in animals with power of self-movement it is very natural that the young should
remain with the old, if no external circumstances
supply a ground for them to remove themselves.
The living together of individuals of the same
species, the most primitive form of social life, is
also the most primitive forms of life itself. The
division of organisms, which have a common
origin, is a later act.

The separation can be brought about by the
most diverse causes. The most obvious, and
certainly the most effective, is the lack of sustenance. Each locality can only yield a certain
quantity of food. If a certain species of animals
multiplies beyond the limits of their food supply,
the superfluous ones must either emigrate or
starve. Above a certain number the numbers of
organisms living in one place can not go.

But there are certain species of animals, for
whom the isolation, the division in individual
pairs, who live only for themselves, for whom
such a life affords an advantage in the struggle
for existence. Thus, for example, for the cat
species, which lie in wait for their booty and take
it with an unexpected spring. This method of
acquiring their sustenance would be made more
difficult, if not impossible, if they circulated in
herds. The first spring on the booty would drive
all the game away for all the others. For wolves

which do not come unexpectedly on their prey, but worry it to death, the foregathering in herds affords an advantage; one hunts the game to the other, which blocks for it the way. The cat nevertheless hunts more successfully alone.

On the other hand again there are animals who choose isolation because in this fashion they are less conspicuous and can easiest hide themselves, soonest escape the foe. The traps set by man have, for example, had the effect that many animals which formerly lived in societies, are now only to be found isolated, such as the beavers in Europe. That is the only way for them to remain unnoticed.

On the other hand, however, there are numerous animals which draw advantage from their social life. They are seldom beasts of prey. We have mentioned the wolf above. But even they only hunt in bands when food is scarce, in winter. In summer when it is easier to get, they live in pairs. The nature of the beast of prey is always inclined to fighting and violence, and consequently does not agree well with its equals.

The herbivora are more peaceful from the very manner in which they obtain their food. That very fact of itself renders it easier for them to herd together, or to remain together, because they are more defenceless, they win, however, through their greater numbers, new weapons in the struggle for life. The union of many weak forces in common action can produce a new and greater force. Then through union the greater strength of certain individuals is used for the good of all. When the stronger ones fight now for themselves, they fight for the good of the weaker, when the more experienced look out for their own safety, find out for themselves feeding grounds, they do it also for the inexperienced. Now it becomes possible to introduce a division of labor among the united individuals, fleeting though it be, yet it increases their strength and their safety. It is impossible to watch the neighborhood with the most complete attention and at the same time to feed peacefully. Naturally during sleep all observation of all kind comes to an end. But in society one watcher suffices to render the others safe during sleep or while eating.

Through the division of labors the union of individuals becomes a body with different organs to coöperate to a given end, and this end is the maintenance of the collective body; it becomes an organism. This is by no means to say that the new organism, society, is a body in the same way as an animal or a plant, but it is an organism of its own kind, which is far more widely distinguished from those two than the animal from the plant. Both are made up from cells without power of self motion and without consciousness of their own; society on the other hand from individuals with their own power of movement and consciousness. If, however, the animal organism has, as a whole, a power of self motion and consciousness, they are lacking nevertheless to society as well as to the plant. But the individuals which form the society can entrust individuals among their members with functions through which the social forces are submitted to a uniform will, and uniform movements in the society are produced.

On the other hand the individual and society are much looser connected than the cell and the whole organism, in both plant and animal. The individuals can separate itself from one society and join another as emigration proves. That is impossible for a cell; for it the separation from the whole is death, if we leave certain cells of a particular kind out of account, such as the sperma and eggs in the procreative processes. Again society can forthwith impose on new individuals any change of form, without any change of substance, which is impossible for an animal body. Finally the individuals who form society can, under circumstances, change the organs and organization of society, while anything of that kind is quite impossible in an animal or vegetable organism.

If, therefore, society is an organism, it is no

animal organism, and to attempt to explain any
phenomena peculiar to society from the laws of
the animal organism is not less absurd than when
the attempt is made to deduce peculiarities of the
animal organism, such as self movement and
consciousness, from the laws of vegetable being.
Naturally this does not say there is not also
something common to the various kinds of organisms.

Just as the animal, so will also the social organism survive so much the better in the struggle
for existence the more unitary its movements, the
stronger the binding forces, the greater the harmony of the parts. But society has no fixed
skeleton, which supports the weaker parts, no
skin which covers the whole, no circulation of
the blood which nourishes all the parts, no heart
which regulates it, no brain which makes a unity
out of its knowing, its working and its movements. Its unity and harmony, as well as the
coherence can only arise from the actions and
will of its members. This unitary will will, however, be so much the more assured the more it
springs from a strong impulse.

Among species of animals, in whom the social
bond becomes a weapon in the struggle for life,
this encourages consequently social impulses
which in many species and many individuals
grow to an extraordinary strength, so that they

can overcome the impulse of self preservation and reproduction when they come in conflict with the same.

The commencement of the social impulse we can well look for in the interest which the simple fact of living together in society produces in the individuals for his fellows, to whose society he is accustomed from youth on. On the other hand reproduction and care for the progeny already render longer or shorter relations of a more intimate kind necessary between different individuals of the same species. And just as these relations have formed the starting point for the formation of societies, so could the corresponding impulses easily give the point of departure for the development of the social impulses.

These impulses themselves can vary according to the varying conditions of the various species, but a row of impulses forms the requisite conditions for the growth of any kind of society. In the first place naturally comes altruism, self sacrifice for the whole. Then bravery in the defence of the common interests; fidelity to the community; submission to the will of society; then obedience and discipline; truthfulness to society whose security is endangered or whose energies are wasted when they are misled in any way by false signals. Finally ambition, the sensibility to the praise and blame of society. These all are social impulses which we find expressed already among animal societies, many of them in a high degree.

These social impulses are nevertheless nothing but the highest virtues, they sum up the entire moral code. At the most they lack the love for justice, that is the impulse for equality. For its development there certainly is no place in the animal societies, because they only know natural and individual inequality, and not those called forth by social relations, the social inequalities. The lofty moral law, that the comrade ought never to be merely a means to an end, which the Kantians look on as the most wonderful achievement of Kant's genius, and as the moral programme of the modern era, and for the entire future history of the world, that is in the animal world a commonplace. The development of human society first created a state of affairs in which the companion became a simple tool of others.

What appeared to a Kant as the creation of a higher world of spirits, is a product of the animal world. How narrowly the social impulses have grown up with the fight for existence, and to what an extent they originally were useful in the preservation of species, can be seen from the fact that their effect often limits itself to individuals whose maintenance is advantageous to the species. Quite a number of animals, which risk their lives to save younger or weaker comrades, kill without a scruple sick or aged comrades who are superfluous for the preservation of the race, and are become a burden to society. The "moral sense," "sympathy," does not extend to these elements. Even many savages behave like that.

An animal impulse and nothing else is the moral law. Thence comes its mysterious nature this voice in us which has no connection with any external impulse, or any apparent interest this demon or god, which since Socrates and Plato, those moralists found in themselves who refused to deduce morality from self love or pleasure. Certainly a mysterious impulse, but not more mysterious than sexual love, the maternal love, the instinct of self preservation, the being of the organism itself and so many other things, which only belong to the world of phenomena and which no one looks on as products of a supersensuous world.

Because the moral law is the universal instinct of equal force to the instinct of self preservation and reproduction, thence its force, thence its power which we obey without thought, thence our rapid decisions, in particular cases, whether an action is good or bad, virtuous or vicious thence the energy and decision of our moral judgment, and thence the difficulty to prove it when reason begins to analyze its grounds. Then one finally finds that to comprehend all means to pardon all, that everything is necessary, that nothing is good and bad.

Not from our organs of knowing, but from our impulses comes the moral law and the moral judgment as well as the feeling of duty and the conscience.

In many kinds of animals the social impulses attain such a strength, that they become stronger than all the rest. Do the former come in conflict with the latter, they then confront the latter with overpowering strength as commands of duty. Nevertheless that does not hinder in such a case a special impulse, say of self preservation or of reproduction being temporarily stronger than the social impulse and overcoming it. But is the danger past, then the strength of the self preserving impulse or the reproductive instinct shrivels up, just as that of reproduction after the completion of the act. The social instinct remains however, existing in the old force, regains the dominion over the individual and works now in him as the voice of conscience and of repentance. Nothing is more mistaken than to see in conscience the voice of fright of his fellows, their opinion or even their power of physical compulsion. It has effect even in respect of acts, which no one has heard of, even acts which appear to the neighbors very praiseworthy, it can even work as repugnance of acts which have been undertaken from fear of his fellows and their public opinion.

Public opinion, praise and blame are certainly very influential factors. But their effect assumes in advance a certain social impulse, namely, ambition, they cannot produce the social impulses.

We have no reason to assume that conscience is confined to man. We would find it difficult to find even in men, if everyone did not feel its effect on himself. Conscience is certainly a force, which does not obviously and openly show itself, but works only in the innermost being.

But nevertheless many investigators have gone so far as to posit even in animals a kind of conscience. Thus says Darwin in his book "The Descent of Man."

"Besides Love and Sympathy the animals show other qualities connected with the social instincts, which we should call moral in men; and I agree with Agassiz that dogs have something very like a conscience. Dogs certainly have a certain power of self control, and this does not appear to be altogether a consequence of fear. As Braubach remarks, a dog will restrain itself from stealing food in the absence of its master."

If conscience and feeling of duty are a consequence of the lasting predominance of the social impulses in many species of animals, if these impulses are those through which the individuals of such species are the most constantly and most enduringly determined, while the force of the other impulses is subject to great oscillations, yet the force of the social impulse is not free from all oscillations. One of the most peculiar phenomena is that social animals, when united in greater numbers, also feel stronger social impulses. It is for example a well known fact that an entirely different spirit reigns in a well filled meeting then in a weak, that the bigger crowd alone has an inspiring effect on the speaker. In a crowd the individuals are not only more brave, that could be explained through the greater support which each believes he will get from his fellows; they are also more unselfish, more self sacrificing, more enthusiastic. Certainly then only too often so much the more calculating, cowardly and selfish when they find themselves alone. And that applies not only in men but also in the social animals. Thus Espinas, in his book, "Animal Societies," quotes an observation of Forel. The latter found:

"The courage of every ant, by the same form, increases in exact proportion to the number of its companions or friends, and decreases in exact proportion the more isolated it is from its companions. Every inhabitant of a very populous ant heap, is much more courageous than a similar one from a small population. The same female worker, which will allow herself to be killed ten times in the midst of her companions, will show itself extraordinarily timid, avoid the least danger, fly before even a much weaker ant so soon as she finds herself twenty steps from her own home."

With the stronger social feeling there need not necessarily be bound up a higher faculty of intelligence. In general every instinct probably has the effect to somewhat obscure the exact observation of the external world. What we wish, that we readily believe, but what we fear that we easily exaggerate. The instincts have the effect that very easily many things appear disproportionately big or near, while others are overlooked. How blind and deaf the instinct for reproduction can render many animals at times is well known. The social instincts which do not show themselves as a rule so acutely and intensively, generally obscure much less the intellectual faculties. They can, however, influence them very considerably on occasions. Think, for instance, on the influence of faithfulness, and discipline among sheep, who follow their leading sheep blindly, wherever it may go.

The moral law in us can lead our intellect

astray just as any other impulse. In itself it is
neither a product of wisdom nor does it produce
wisdom. What is apparently the most elevated
and divine in us, is essentially the same as that
which we look on as the commonest and most
devilish. The moral law is of the same nature as
the instinct for reproduction. Nothing is more
ridiculous, than when the former is put on a ped-
estal and the latter is turned away with loathing
and contempt. But no less false is it to infer that
man can and ought to follow all his instincts
without check. That is only so far true as it is
impossible to condemn any one of these as such.
But that by no means implies that they cannot
come to cross purposes. It is simply impossible
that any one should follow all his instincts without restraint, because they restrain one another.
Which, however, at a given moment wins, and
what consequences this victory brings for the
individual and his society with it, there neither
the Ethic of pleasure nor that of a moral law
standing outside of space and time affords us
any help.

If, however, the moral law is recognized as
a social impulse, which like all the impulses is
brought out in us by the struggle for life, the
supersensuous world has lost a strong support in human thinking. The simple gods of
Polytheism were already dethroned by natural

Philosophy.   If nevertheless a new Philosophy could arise which not only reawakened the belief in God and a supersensuous world but put it more firmly on a higher form, as was done in ancient times by Plato, and on the eve of the French Revolution by Kant, so did the cause lie in the unsolved problem of the moral law, to whose explanation neither its deduction from pleasure nor from the moral sense sufficed — and yet these offered the only " natural " causal explanation which seemed possible. Darwinism was the first to make an end to the division of man, which this rendered necessary, into a natural and animal on the one hand and a supernatural heavenly, on the other.

But with that was the entire ethical problem not yet solved. Were moral impulse, duty and conscience as well as the ground type of the virtues to be explained from the social impulse, yet this breaks down when it is a question of explaining the moral idea. Of that there is not the least sign in the animal world. Only man can set himself ideals and follow them. Whence come these? Are they prescribed to the human race from the beginning of all time as an irrevocable demand of nature or an eternal Reason, as commands which man does not produce but which confront man as a ruling force and show him the aims toward which he has ever

more and more to strive? That was in the
main the view of all thinkers of the 18th century, atheists as well as theists, materialists and
idealists. This view took even in the mouth of
the boldest materialism the tendency to assume
a supernatural Providence, which indeed had
nothing more to do in nature but still hovers over
human society. The evolution idea which recognized the descent of man from the animal world
made this kind of idealism absurd in a materialistic mouth.

All the same before Darwin founded his epoch-
making work that theory had arisen which revealed the secret of the moral ideal. It was the
theory of Marx and Engels.

CHAPTER V

THE ETHICS OF MARXISM

1. THE ROOTS OF THE MATERIALIST CONCEPTION OF HISTORY.

The rapid progress of the natural sciences since the French Revolution is intimately connected with the expansion of capitalism from that time on. The capitalist big industry rests more and more on the application of science and consequently had every reason to supply it with men and means. The modern technic gives to science not only new objects of activity but also new tools and new methods. The international communication finally brought new material to it. Thus it acquired strength and means to carry the idea of evolution successfully through.

But even more than for natural science was the French Revolution an epoch of importance for the Science of society, the so-called mental sciences. Because in natural science the idea of evolution had already given a great stimulus to many thinkers. In mental science on the other hand it was only to be found in the most rudimentary attempts. Only after the French Revolution could it develop in them.

The mental sciences — Philosophy, Law, History, Political Economy — had been for the rising Bourgeoisie before the French Revolution in the first place a means of fighting the ruling powers, social and political, which opposed them and had their roots in the past. To discredit the past, and to paint the new and coming in contrast to it, as the only good and useful, that formed the principal occupation of these sciences.

That has altered since the Revolution. This gave the Bourgeoisie the essence of what they wanted. It revealed to them, however, social forces which wanted to go further than themselves. These new forces began to be more dangerous than the relics of the deposed old. To come to an agreement with the latter became only a requirement of political sagacity on the part of the Bourgeoisie. Therewith, however, their opinion on the past was bound also to grow milder.

On the other hand the Revolution had brought a great disillusionment to the Ideologues themselves. Great as were its achievements for the Bourgeoisie, they were not up to the expectations of a harmonious empire of " morality," general well being, and happiness, such as had been looked for from the overthrow of the old. No one dared to build hopes on the new; the more unsatisfactory the present, so much the more terrifying were the reminiscences of the most recent past which the present had brought to a head, so much the more bright did the farther past appear. That produced as is well known Romanticism in art. But it produced also similar movements in the mental sciences. Men began to study the past, not in order to condemn it, but to understand it; not to show up its absurdity, but to understand its reasonableness.

But the Revolution had done its work too thoroughly for men to dream of re-establishing what had been set aside. Had the past been rational, so it was necessary to see that it had become irrational. The socially necessary and reasonable ceased with that to appear as an unchangeable conception. Thus arose the view of a social evolution.

That applied first to the knowledge of German History. In Germany the above described process was most markedly to be seen. The revolutionary method of thought had never penetrated so deeply, had never struck such deep roots as in France, the Revolution had not worked so thoroughly, had shaken the forces and opinions of the past in a less degree, and finally had appeared on the scene more as a disturbing than an emancipating element.

But to the study of the German past there as-
sociated itself the investigation of similar periods.
In America the young community of the United
States was already so far advanced, that there a
separate class of intellectuals had already developed a real American literature and science.
What specially distinguished America from Europe, was, however, the close contact of the capitalist civilization of the white man with Indian
barbarism. That was the object which especially
attracted literature and sciences. Soon after the
German romanticism there arose the American
Indian romance and soon after the rise of the
historical school of law, the revival of the old
fairy tales and the world of legends, and the comparative philological research in Germany, the
scientific theory of the social and linguistic conditions of the Indians in America.

At an earlier period, however, the settlement
of the English in India had afforded the possibility, nay, the necessity, of a study of the
languages, the customs, the laws of these territories. At the commencement of the nineteenth
century the knowledge of Sanscrit had penetrated as far as Germany, which laid the foundation for the comparative study of languages,
which in its turn afforded the most valuable
insight into the life of the Indo-Germanic
peoples in primitive times. All this rendered it

possible to treat the accounts given by civilized observers on primitive peoples as well as the discoveries of weapons and tools of disappeared races differently from formerly when they had been simply looked on as curiosities. They now became material to prolong the already revealed parts of human development still further into the past and to close up many of the gaps.

In this entire historical work there was, however, lacking the object which had up to then ruled the entire writing of history —the distinguished human individual. In the written sources, from which formerly the knowledge of human history was exclusively culled, only the extraordinary had been related, because it was that only which seemed noteworthy to the chronicler of the events of his time. Who cared to describe what was everyday, what everybody knew! The extraordinary man, the extraordinary event, such as wars and revolutions, alone seemed worth relating. Thus it was that for the traditional historians, who never got beyond writing up from the sources handed down to them with more or less criticism, the big man was the motor power in history; in the feudal period the king, the military commander, the religious founder, and the priests. In the eighteenth century these very men were branded by the Bourgeois intellectuals as the authors of all the evil

in the world, and the philosophers on the other
hand as legislators and teachers, as the only real
instruments of progress. But all progress appears to be only external, or simple change of
clothes. That period in which the sources of historical writing began to flow more abundantly,
the time of the victory of the Greeks over the
Persian Invasion, was the culminating period of
the social development. From that time on society in the lands round the Mediterranean began
to decay, it went down and down till the Barbarian Immigration. Only slowly have the peoples of Europe since then developed themselves
again to a higher level socially, and even in the
18th century they had not risen far above the
lead of classical antiquity, so that in many points
of politics, of philosophy, and especially of art
the latter could rank as a pattern.

History, as a whole, appeared simply as a rise
and descent, a repetition of the same circle; and
just as the simple individual can set himself
continually higher aims than he arrives at, because as a rule he fails, so did this circle appear
as a horrible tragi-comedy in which all that was
most elevated and strongest was doomed to play
wretched parts.

Quite otherwise was it with primitive history.
That with its individual departments, History of
Law, Comparative Philology, Ethnology, found in

the material which they worked up, not the extraordinary and the individual but the every day and commonplace described. But for that very reason can primitive history trace with certainty a line of continuous development. And the more her material grows, the more it is possible to compare like with like, the more it is discovered that this development is no chance, but according to law. The material which is at our disposal is on the one side facts of the technical arrangements of life, on the other of law, custom and religion. To them the law controlling this means nothing else than to bring technics into a causal connection with the legal, moral, and religious conceptions without the help of extraordinary individuals or events.

This connection was, however, discovered almost simultaneously from another side, namely statistics.

So long as the Parish was the most important economic institution, statistics were hardly required. In the Parish it was easy to get a view of the state of affairs. But even if statistics were made there, they could scarcely suggest scientific observations, as with such small figures the law had no chance of showing itself. That was bound to alter, as the capitalist method of production created the modern states, which were not, like the earlier, simple bundles of communes or parishes and provinces, but unitary bodies with important economic functions.

Besides that, however, the capitalist method of production developed the state not simply to the inner market, but beside that created the world market. That produced highly complicated connections which were not to be controlled without the means of statistics. Founded for the practical purpose of tax gathering and raising of recruits, for customs, and finally for the Insurance societies, it gradually embraced wider and wider spheres and produced a mass of observations on a large scale, which showed laws which must impress themselves on observant compilers of the material. In England this happened at the end of the 17th century, when Petty arrived at a political arithmetic, in which, however, "estimates" played a very big rôle. At the beginning of the nineteenth century the method of statistical enquiries was so complete and its sphere so varied that it was possible to discover with the greatest certainty the laws governing the actions of great masses of men. The Belgian Quetelet made an attempt in the thirties, to describe in this manner the physiology of human society.

They saw that the determining element in the alterations of human action was always a material change, usually an economic one. Thus was the decrease and increase of crime, of suicide, marriages, shown to be dependent on the prices of corn.

Not as if economic motives were for instance the sole cause that marriages were made at all. Nobody would declare the sexual passion to be an economic motive. But the alteration in the annual number of marriages is called forth by changes in the economic situation.

Besides all these new sciences there is finally to be mentioned a change in the character of the modern writing of history. The French Revolution came to the fore so clearly as a class-struggle, that not only its historian must recognize that, but a number of the historians were inspired to investigate in other periods of history the role of the class wars, and to see in them the motive forces of human development. The classes are, however, again a product of the economic structure of society, and from this spring the antagonisms, therefore the struggles of the classes. What holds every class together, what divides them from other classes, determines their opposition to men, is the particular class interests, a new kind of interest, about which no moralist of the eighteenth century had had any idea whatever school he might belong to.

With all these advances and discoveries which certainly often enough were only piece-

meal and by no means quite clear by the time of
the forties in the nineteenth century all the essential elements of the materialist conception of
history had been supplied. They only waited for
the master who should bring them under control
and unify them. That was done by Engels and
Marx.

Only to deep thinkers such as they were was
an achievement of that nature possible, in so far
that was their personal work. But no Engels,
no Marx could have achieved it in the 18th century, before all the new sciences had produced a
sufficient mass of new results. On the other
hand a man of the genius of a Kant or a Helvetius could also have discovered the materialist
conception of history if at their time the requisite
scientific conditons had been at hand. Finally,
however, even Engels and Marx despite their
genius and despite the preparatory work, which
the new sciences had achieved, would not have
been able even in the time of the forties in the
19th century, to discover it, if they had not
stood on the standpoint of the proletariat, and
were thus socialists. That also was absolutely
necessary to the discovery of this conception of
history. In this sense is it a proletariat philosophy and the opposing views are Bourgeois phi-
losophies.

The rise of the idea of evolution took place

during a period of reaction, when no immediate farther development of society was in question; the conception consequently only served for the explanation of the previous development, and thereby only in a certain sense, that of a justification, nay, at times more, a glorification of the past. Just as through Romanticism and the historical school of jurisprudence, there goes through the entire study of early times, even through Sanscrit study — I may point to the example of Schopenhauer's Buddhism — in the first decades of the last century a reactionary trait. So was it with that philosophy which made the evolutionary idea of that period the centre of its system, the Hegelian. Even that was only intended to be a panegyric on the previous development, which had now found its close in the monarchs by the will of God. As a reactionary philosophy this philosophy of the development was bound to be an idealist philosophy, since the present, the reality, was in too great a contradiction with its reactionary tendencies.

As soon as reality, that is the capitalist society, had got so far as to be able to make itself felt in face of these tendencies, the idealist conception of evolution became impossible. It was superseded by a more or less open materialism. But only from the proletariat point of view was it possible to translate the social development into a materialistic one—in other words to recogrize in the present an evolution of society proceeding according to natural laws.

The Bourgeoisie was obliged to close its eyes to all idea of a further social evolution, and repudiate every philosophy of evolution, which did not simply investigate the development of the part to understand this, but also in order to understand the tendencies of the new society of the future and to hammer out weapons for the struggle of the present, which is destined to bring about this form of society of the future.

So soon as this period of intellectual reaction after the great Revolution had been overcome, and the Bourgeoisie which had regained self respect and power had made an end to all artistic and philosophic romanticism in order to proclaim materialism, they could not all the same get as far as the historic materialism. Deeply founded as this was in the circumstances of the time, so was it no less in the nature of the circumstances, that that could only be a philosophy of the proletariat, that it was repudiated by science so far as it lay in the influence of the Bourgeoisie, repudiated to such an extent that even the socialist author of the history of materialism, Albert Lange, only mentions Karl Marx in that work as an economist and not as a philosopher.

The idea of evolution, generally accepted for

the natural sciences, even fruitful for certain special branches of mental science, has remained dead for the sciences as a whole as taught by Bourgeois science. The Bourgeoisie could not even get further than Hegel in their philosophy. They fell back into a materialism which stands considerably below that of the 18th century, because it is purely natural philosophy, and has no theory of society to show. And when this narrow materialism no longer suited them, they turned to the old Kantianism, purified from all the defects which had been superseded by science in the meantime, but not emancipated from its Ethic which was now the bulwark which was to be brought against the materialist theory of Social Evolution.

In the economic sciences the Bourgeoisie hovered between a historic conception which certainly acknowledges an evolution of society, but denies necessary laws of this development, and a view which recognizes necessary laws of Society but denies the social development and believes it possible to discover in the psychology of primitive man all the economic categories of modern society. To this conception there was added a naturalistic (or natural scientific) which tries to reduce the laws of society to laws of biology, that is, to the laws of animal and plant organisms, and really amounts to nothing short of a denial of social development.

Since the Bourgeoisie has grown conservative, only from the proletarian standpoint is a materialist view of social development possible.

It is true that the dialectical materialism is a materialism of its own kind, which is quite different from the materialism of natural science (naturalism). Many friends have wished accordingly in order to avoid misunderstandings, to substitute another word for the word materialism.

But if Marx and Engels held on to the word materialism that had the same ground as the refusal to rechristian their manifesto of the Communists into a manifesto of the Socialists. The word socialism covers today such various wares, among them some really worthless, Christian and national socialisms of all kinds; the word communism on the other hand describes unmistakably and clearly the aims of a proletariat fighting a revolutionary fight for its emancipation.

So also by a designation of the dialetical materialism as dialectical " monism," or " Criticism " or " Realism " were its significance as opposition to the Bourgeois world lost. The word " materialism " on the other hand has signified since the victory of Christianity a philosophy of the fight against the ruling powers. Therefore has it come into disrepute with the Bourgeoisie, but for that very reason have we followers of the proletarian philosophy every reason to hold fast to this very name, which also can be justified in fact. And a conception of Ethics, which rises from this philosophy can rank as a materialistic one.

II. THE ORGANIZATION OF HUMAN SOCIETY.

a. The Technical Development.

Let us now regard man from the standpoint of the materialist conception of history at the stage at which we left him in the last chapter, at the boundary which divided him from the rest of the animal world. What is it that raises him above it? Do there exist between him and them only gradual differences or is there also an essential difference? Neither as a thinking nor as a moral being is man essentially different from the animals. Does not perhaps the difference lie in the fact that he *produces*, that is, adapts material found in nature by means of change of form or of place to his purposes? This activity is, however, also found in the animal world. To leave out of account many insects, such as bees and ants we find among many warm blooded animals, nay, even among many fishes, species of productive activity, namely, the production of refuges and dwellings, with underground buildings, and so on. And, however much of this productive activity is also the product and result of inherited instincts and the positions, they are often so suitably adapted to various circumstances, that consciousness, the knowledge of causal connections, must also play a part thereby.

Or is it the use of tools which raises man above the animals? Also note that among animals we find at least the beginnings of the appliation of tools, of branches, of trees for defence, of stones for cracking nuts and so on. This intelligence as well as the development of the feet to hands enables the apes to do that.

Thus not the production of means of consumption and not the use of tools distinguishes man from the animals. What, however, alone distinguishes the former is the production of tools, which serve for production, for defence or attack. The animal can at the most find the tool in nature: it is not capable of inventing such. It may produce things for its immediate use, prepare dwellings, collect provisions but it does not think so far as to produce things which will not serve for direct consumption, but the production of the means of consumption.

With the production of the means of production the animal man begins to become the human man; with that he breaks away from the animal world to found his own empire, an empire with its own kind of development, which is wholly unknown in the rest of nature, in which nothing similar is to be found.

So long as the animal only produces with the organs provided by nature, or only uses tools which nature gives him, it cannot rise above the means thus provided for them by nature. His development only occurs in the manner that his own organism develops itself, his own organs unfold themselves — the brain included: a slow and unconscious process carried on by means of the struggle for life, which the animal can in no way hurry on by its conscious activity.

On the other hand the discovery and production of the tool — the word employed in the widest sense — means that man consciously and purposely gives himself new organs, or strengthens or lengthens his natural organs, so that he can still better or easier produce the same that these organs produced, but besides that he is in a position to arrive at results which were formerly quite unattainable for him. But as man is not simply an animal endowed with higher intelligence and hands — the necessary assumption of the application and production of tools, — but also must have been from the very beginning a social animal, the discovery and production of a tool by a specially gifted individual — a Marx

or Kant or Aristotle inhabiting the trees of the
primitive tropical forests who had found it —
was not lost with his death. His herd took up
the invention and carried it on, won with it an
advantage in the struggle for life, so that their
descendants could flourish better than the other
members of their kind. But further perspicacity
which was to be found in the herd served the
purpose from now on of rendering the discovery
more complete or to invent new things.

Even if a certain degree of intelligence and
the development of the hand forms the necessary
condition for the discovery. and production of
tools, so the social character of man afforded
the conditions for the continual addition of new
and the improvement of old discoveries, thus
leading to a continual development of the technic.
The slow and unconscious process of the development of the individuals through the struggle
for life, as it ruled the entire remaining organic
world, gives way more and more in the human
world in favour of the conscious transformation,
adaptation and improvement of the organs, a
development which in its beginning, measured by
modern standards, is extremely slow and hard to
notice, but which all the same goes much quicker
than the natural selection. The technical progress forms from now on the foundation of the
entire development of man. On that and not on

any special divine spark rests all by which man is distinguished from the animals.

Every single step forwards on this path of technical development is a conscious and intentional. Each arises from the endeavor to increase the powers of man over the limits set by nature. But each of these technical advances brings also of necessity effects with it, which were not intended by its authors and could not be, because they were not in a position even to expect them, effects, which just as much as natural selection could be called adaption to the surroundings, surroundings, however, which men had artificially modified. In these adaptations, however, consciousness, the knowledge of the new surroundings, and its requirements, again plays a rôle, this nevertheless is not that of an independent directory force.

b. Technic and Method of Life.

Let us seek, in order to get a clearer idea of what has been said, to give ourselves an idea what consequences it was bound to have when primitive man arrived at the first tool, where he joined the stone and the stick, which the ape had already used, to make a hammer, an axe or a spear. Naturally the description which here follows can only be a hypothetical one, as we have no witness of the whole process. But it is not to serve as a proof, only as an illustration. We make it as simple as possible, disregarding for example the influence which the fishing could have had on primitive man.

So soon as primitive man possessed the spear, he was put in a position to hunt still bigger animals. Was his food up to then principally from tree fruits and insects, as well as probably little birds and young birds, now he could kill even bigger animals, meat became from now on more important for his food. The majority of the bigger animals, however, live on the earth, not in the trees, hunting thus drew him from his airy regions down to the earth. Still more. The animals most adapted for the chase, the ruminants, are rare in the primitive forest. The more man became a hunter, the more could he emerge from the forest in which primitive man was hid.

This account, as I have said, is purely hypothetical. The process of evolution may have been the reverse. Equally as the discovery of the tool and the weapons could have driven men out of the primitive forest to draw forth into open grass land where the trees were farther apart, just as well might forces which drove primitive man from his original abode have been the spur to the discovery of weapons and tools. 'Let us assume, for instance, that the number of men increased over their means of subsistence in a glacial period, say the glacier of the central Asiatic mountain range sank low down and forced the inhabitants from their forests into the grass plains which bordered it or that an increasing dryness of the climate ever more and more cleared the forest and caused more and more grass land to come up in it. In all these cases primitive man would have been obliged to give up his free life and to move about on the earth; he was obliged from now on to seek for animal food, and could no longer in the same degree feed himself from tree fruits. The new method of life induced him to use often stones and sticks and brought him nearer to the discovery of the first tools and weapons.

Whatever development we accept, the first or the second — and both could have taken place independent of each other at different points — from both of them we see clearly the close connection which exists between new means of production and new methods of life and new needs.

Each of these factors necessarily produces the other, each becomes necessarily the cause of changes, which in their turn hide new fresh changes in their bosom. Thus every discovery produces inevitable changes, which give rise to other discoveries, and therewith brings new needs and methods of life which again call forth new discoveries and so on — a chain of endless development which becomes so much quicker and complicated, the farther it proceeds and the more the possibility and facility of new discoveries grows.

Let us consider the consequences which the rise of hunting as a source of food for man and his emergence from the primitive forest was bound to draw with it.

Besides the meat, man took in place of the tree fruits, roots and fruits of the grasses, corn and maize into his bill of fare. In the primitive forest a cultivation of plants is impossible and to clear the primitive forest is beyond the power of primitive man. The latter could not, however, even arrive at this idea. He lived from tree fruits; to plant fruit trees which would first bear fruit after many years assumes that already a high degree of culture and settlement has been attained. On the other hand the planting of grasses in meadows and steppes is much easier than in the primitive forest and can be brought about with much simpler tools. The thought of planting grasses, which often bear fruits after only a few weeks, is, however, easier conceivable than that of planting trees. Cause and effect are so nearly connected in this case that their dependence is easier to see and even the unsettled primitive man might expect to be be able to hope to be able to hold out the period between seed time and harvest in the neighborhood of the cultivated ground.

On the other hand man so soon as he left the primitive forest was far more at the mercy of climatic changes than in his primitive home. In the thick forest the changes of temperature between day and night are much less than on the open plain, on which during the day a burning sun rules and by night a powerful radiation and loss of heat. Storms are also less noticeable in the forest than in a woodless territory, and against rain and hail this latter offers much less protection than the almost impenetrable foliage of the forest. Thus man forced on to the plains was bound to feel a need for shelter and clothing which the primitive man in the tropical forest never felt. If the man apes had already built themselves formal nests for the night repose he was bound to go farther and build walls and roofs for protection, or to seek shelter in caves or holes. On the other hand it was no great step to clothe himself in the skins of animals, which remained over after the flesh had been taken out of them. It was certainly the need for protection against cold which allowed mankind to aspire for the possession of fire. Its technical ability he could only gradually learn after he had used it a long time. The warmth which it gave out was on the other hand at once evident. How

man came to the use of fire will perhaps never be
certainly known.   But it is certain that man in
the primitive forest had no need for it as a
source of heat, and was not able amid the continual damp to maintain it.   Only in a drier region,   where   greater   quantities   of   dry   fire
material   were   to   be   found   at   intervals,   moss,
leaves, brushwood, could fires arise which made.
man acquainted with fire.   Perhaps through lightning   or   more   likely   from   the   sparks   of   a   flint,
the first tool of primitive man, or from the heat
which arose from boring holes in hard wood.

We see how the entire life of man, his needs,
his   dwelling,   his   means   of   sustenance   were
changed, and one discovery finally brought numerous others in its train, so soon as it was once
made, so soon as the making of a spear or an
axe had been achieved.   In all these transforma-
tions consciousness played a great part, but the
consciousness   of   other   generations   than   those
which had discovered the spear or the axe.   And
the tasks which were presented to the consciousness of the later generations, were not set by
that of the former, they arose by necessity and
spontaneously as soon as the discovery was made.

But   with   the   change   of   dwelling,   of   the   needs
of the winning of sustenance, of the entire method of life, are the effects of the discovery not
exhausted.

c. *Animal and Social Organism.*

The division of labour among the organs in the animal organism has certain limits, since they are hide bound to the animal organism, and cannot be changed at pleasure and their number is limited. On the other hand a limit is herewith set for the variety of the functions which an animal organism is capable of performing. It is, for instance, impossible that the same limb should serve equally well for holding things, for running and for flying, not to speak of other specializations.

The tool on the other hand can be changed by man. He can adapt it to a simple definite purpose. Is this fulfilled then he puts it on one side, it does not hinder him in other work for which he requires quite other tools. If the number of his limbs is limited, his tools are innumerable.

But not simply the number of the organs of the animal organism is limited, but also the force with which any of them can be moved. It can be in no case greater than the strength of the individual himself, to whom they belong, they must always be less, since it has to nourish all its organs besides the one in motion. On the other hand, the force which moves a tool is by no means confined to one individual. So soon as it is separated from the human individual, many individuals can unite to operate it, nay, they can use other than human forces for the purpose, say the beasts of burden, again water, wind or steam.

Thus in contrast to the animal organism the development of the artificial organs of man is unlimited, at least measured by human ideas. They find their limit only in the mass of the moving forces, which Sun and Earth place at the disposal of man.

The separation of the artificial organs of man from his personality has, however, still other effects. If the organs of the animal organisms are bound up with it, that means that every individual has the same organs at his disposal. The sole exception is formed by the organs of reproduction. Only in this region is a division of labour to be found among the higher organisms. Every other division of labour in the animal organism rests simply on the fact that certain individuals take over certain functions for a certain period, for example, the sentry duty, as leader, etc., without requiring for the purpose organs which are different to those of other individuals.

The discovery of the tool on the other hand made it possible that in a society certain individuals should exclusively use certain tools or any way so much oftener that they understand its use far better than any one else. Thus we come to a form of division of labour in human society, which is of quite another kind from the modest beginnings of such in the animal societies. In the latter there remains, with all the division of labour a being by itself, which possesses all the organs, which it requires for its support. In human society that is less the case, the farther the division of labour advances in it. The more developed is this, so much the greater the number of the organs which society has at its disposal for the gaining of their sustenance and the maintenance of their method of life, but so much the greater also the number of the organs, which are required, and so much more dependent the organs over which the individual commands. So much the greater the power of society over nature, but so much the more helpless the individual outside of society, so much the more dependent from it. The animal society, which arises as a natural growth, can never raise its members above nature. On the other hand human society forms for the human individual a nature which is a quite peculiar world, apart from the rest, a world which apparently interferes with its being made more than nature, with which latter it imagines itself the better able to cope the more the division of labour increases.

And the latter is practically just as unlimited as the technical progress itself; it finds its limits only in the expansion of the human race.

If we found above, that the animal society is an organism of a peculiar kind, different from the plant and animal, so we now find that the human society again forms a peculiar organism, which is not only different from the plant and animal individual, but is essentially different from the animal society.

Before all there come two distinguishing features into account. We have seen that the animal organism itself possesses all the organs which it requires for its own existence, while the human individual under the advanced division of labour cannot live by itself without society — the Robinson Crusoes, who without any means produce everything for themselves are only to be found in children's story books and scientific works of Bourgeois economists, who believe that the best way to discover the laws of society is to completely ignore it. Man is in his whole nature dependent on society, it rules him, only through the peculiar nature of this is he to be understood.

The peculiar nature of society is, however, in a continual change, because in distinction to the animal society human society is always subject to development in consequence of the advance of their technic. Animal society develops itself probably only in the same degree as the animal species which forms it. Far faster does the process of development proceed in human society. But nothing can be falser than to conceive it according to the nature of the development of the individual, and distinguish the ways of youth, of maturity, of decay and death in it. So long as the sources of force hold out over which the earth commands, therefore so long the foundation of technical progress does not disappear, we have no decay and death of human society to expect, this will, with the advance in technic ever more and more advance and is in this sense immortal.

Every society is modeled by the technical apparatus at its command, and the people who set it going, for which purpose they enter into the complicated social relations. So long as this technical apparatus keeps on improving, and the people who move it, neither diminish in number nor in mental nor physical strength, there can be no talk of a dying out of society.

That sort of thing has never occurred as a permanent condition to any society as yet. Temporarily certainly it occurs, in consequence of peculiarities with which we will make acquaintance later on, that the social relations which sprang from social needs, get petrified and hinder the technical apparatus and the growth of the members of society in number and in intellectual and physical force, nay even give rise to a reactionary movement. That can, however, to speak historically, never last long, sooner or later these fetters of society are burst, either by internal movement, revolutions, or, and what is oftener the case, by impulse from without by wars. Again society changes from time to time a part of its members, its boundaries or its names and it can seem to the observer as if the society had shown traces of old age, and was now dead. In reality, however, if we want to take a simile from the animal organism, it has only been suffering from a disease from which it has everged with renewed strength. Thus did for instance the society of the Roman imperial times not die but rejuvenated through German blood, they began after the migrations of the peoples with partially new people to improve and build up their technical apparatus.

III. THE CHANGES IN THE STRENGTH OF THE SOCIAL INSTINCTS.

a. Language.

Since human society in contrast to the animal is continually changing, for that very reason the people in it must be continually changing. The alteration in the conditions of life must react on the nature of the men, the division of labour necessarily develops some of his natural organs in a greater degree and transforms many. Thus for instance the development of the human ape from a tree fruit eater into a devourer of animals and plants, which are to be found on the ground, was bound to be connected with a transformation of the hind pair of hands into feet. On the other hand, since the discovery of the tool no animal has been subject to such manifold and rapid changes in his natural surroundings as man and no animal confronted with such by an ever growing problem of adaptation to his surroundings as he, and had to use its intellect to the same degree as he. Already at the beginning of that career which he opened with the discovery of the first tool, superior to the rest of the animals by reason of his adaptability and his intellectual powers, he was obliged in the course of his history to encourage both qualities in the highest degree.

If the changes in the society are able to transform the organism of man, his hands, his feet, his brain, how much the more and how much greater to change his consciousness, his views of that which was useful and harmful, good and bad, possible and impossible.

If man begins his rise over the animals with

the discovery of the tool, he has no need to first create a social compact as was believed in the 18th century and as many theoretical jurists still believe in the 20th. He enters on his human development as a social animal, with strong social impulses. The first ethical result of human society could only be to influence the force of these impulses. According to the character of society these impulses will be either strengthened or weakened. There is nothing more false than the idea that the social impulses are bound to be continually strengthened, as society develops.

At the beginning of human society that certainly will have been true. The impulses[which in the animal world had already developed], the social impulses[human society] permits to remain in full strength; it adds further to that — co-operation in work. This co-operation itself has made a new instrument of intercourse of social understanding necessary, language. The social animals could get through, with few means of mutual understanding, cries of persuasion, of joy, of fright, of alarm, of anger and sensational noises. Every individual is with them a whole, which can exist for itself alone. But sensational noises do not, however, suffice, if there is to be common labour or if different tasks are to be allotted, or different products divided. They do not suffice for individuals who are helpless without the help of other individuals. Division of labour is impossible without a language, which describes not merely sensations, but also things and processes, it can only to that degree develop in which language is perfected, and it for its part brings with it the need for it.

In language itself the description of activities and especially the human, is the most primitive; that of the things comes later. The verbs are older than the nouns, the former form the roots from which the latter are derived.

Thus declares Lazarus Geiger:

"When we ask ourselves why light and color were no nameable objects for the first stage of language while the act of painting of the colors was, the answer lies in this that man first only described his actions or those of his kind; he noticed only what happened to himself or in the immediate and to him directly interesting neighborhood, at a period when he had for such things as light and dark, shining objects and lightning no sense and no power of conception. If we take samples from the great number of concepts which we have already touched on (in the book) they go back in their beginning to an extremely limited circle of human movements. For this reason the conception of natural objects evolves in such a remarkably roundabout manner from that conception of a human activity, which in one way or other called attention to them and often brings something that is a distant approximation to them. So the tree is something stripped of its bark, the bark something ground. the corn which grows on it something without the husk. Thus earth and sea, nay even the idea cloud, and heaven itself, emerge from the same root concept of something ground up or painted, a sort of clay-like liquid." (Der Ursprung der Sprache, p. 151–3.)

This way of the development of language is not surprising if we grasp the fact that the first duty of language was the mutual understanding of men in common activities and common movements. This rôle of language as a help in the process of production makes it clear why language had originally so few descriptions of color. Gladstone and others have concluded from that that the Homeric Greeks and other primitive peoples could only distinguish few colors. Nothing more fallacious than that. Experiments have shown that barbarian peoples have a very highly developed sense of color. But their color technic is only little developed, the number of colors which they can produce is small, and hence the number of their descriptions of color is small.

"When man gets so far as to apply a color stuff, then the name of his color stuff easily takes on an adjectival character for him. In this way arise the first names of colors." (Grant Allen, The Color Sense, p. 254.)

Grant Allen points to the fact, that even today the names of colors increase as the color technic grows. The names of the colors serve first the purpose of technic and not the purpose of describing nature.

The development of language is not to be understood without the development of the method of production. From this latter it depends whether a language remains the dialect of a tiny tribe or a world language, which a hundred million men speak.

With the development of language an uncommonly strong means of social cohesion is won, an enormous strengthening and a clear consciousness of the social impulses. In addition it certainly produced quite other effects; it is the most effectual means of retaining acquired knowledge, of spreading this, and handing it on to later generations; it first makes it possible to form concepts, to think scientifically. Thus it starts the development of science and with that brings about the conquest of nature by Science. Now man acquires a mastery over Nature and also an apparent independence of her external influences, which arouse in him the idea of freedom. On this I may be allowed a private deviation. Schopenhauer very rightly says:

The animal has only visual presentations and consequently only motives which it can visualize. The dependence of its acts of will from the motives is thus clear. In men this is no less the case and they are impelled (always taking the individual character into account) by the motive with the strictest necessity: only these are not for the most part visual but abstract presentations, that is conceptions, thoughts which are nevertheless the result of previous views thus of impression from without. That gives him a certain freedom, in comparison namely with the animals. Because he is not like the animal determined by the visual surroundings present before him but by his thoughts drawn from previous experiences or transmitted to him through teaching. Hence the motive which necessarily moves him is not at once clear to the observer with the deed, but he carries it about with him in his head. That gives not only to his actions taken as a whole, but to all his movements an obviously different character from those of the animal; he is at the same time drawn by finer invisible ones. Thus all his movements bear the impress of being guided by principles and intentions, which gives them the appearance of independence and obviously distinguishes them from those of the animal. All these great distinctions depend however entirely from the capacity for abstract presentations, conceptions. (Preisschrift ueber die Grundlage der Moral 1860 p. 148.)

The capacity for abstract presentations depends again on language. Probably it was a deficiency in language which caused the first concept to be formed. In Nature there are only single things; language is, however, too poor to be able to describe every single thing. Man must consequently describe all things which are similar to each other with the same word; he undertakes with that however, at the same time unconsciously a scientific work, the collection of the similar, the separation of the unlike. Language is then not simply an organ of mutual understanding of different men with each other but has become an organ of thinking. Even when we do not speak to others, but think to ourselves only the thoughts must be clothed in certain words.

Does, however, language give man a certain freedom in contrast to the animals, this, all the same, only develops on a higher plane what the formation of the brain had already begun.

In the lower animals the nerves of motion are directly connected with the nerves of sensation; here every external impression at once releases a movement. Gradually, however, a bundle of nerves develops into a centre of the whole nervous system, which receives all the impressions and is not obliged to transmit all to the motor nerves, but can store them up and work them off. The higher animal gathers experiences which it can utilize and impulses which even under certain circumstances it can hand on to its descendants.

Thus through the medium of the brain the connection between the external impression and the movement is obscured. Through language, which renders possible the communication of ideas to others, as well as abstract conceptions, scientific knowledge, and convictions, the connection between sensation and movement becomes in many cases completely unrecognizable.

Something very similar happens in economics. The most primitive form of the circulation of wares is that of barter of commodities: of products which serve for personal or productive consumption. Here from both sides an article of consumption is given and received. The object of the exchange, that is consumption, is clear.

That alters with the rise of an element to facilitate circulation, money. Now it is easy to sell without at once buying, just as the brain makes it possible that impressions should work on the organism without at once releasing a movement. And as this renders possible a storing up of experiences and impulses, which can even be transmitted to descendants, so can notoriously from gold a treasury be collected. And as the collection of that treasury of experiences and impulses under the necessary social conditions finally renders really possible the development of science and the conquest of nature by science, so does the collection of every treasure render possible when certain social conditions are also there the transformation of money into capital, which raises the productivity of human labor in the highest degree and completely revolutionizes the world within a few centuries to a greater degree than formerly occurred in hundreds of thousands of years.

And so just as there are Philosophers who believe that the elements, Brain and Language, intellectual powers and ideas which form the connection between sensation and movement are not simple means to arrange this connection more conveniently for the individual and society, thus apparently to increase their strength, but that they are of themselves sprung from independent sources of power, nay, finally coming even from the creator of the world,—so there are economists who imagine that money brings about the circulation of goods and, as capital, renders it possible to develop human production enormously; that it is this that is the starter of this circulation, the creator of these forces, the producer of all values which are produced over and above the product of the primitive handwork.

The theory of the productivity of capital rests on a process of thought which is very similar to that of the freedom of the will and the conception of a moral law, independent of time and space, which regulates our actions in time and space.

Marx was just as logical when he contradicted the one process of thought as the other.

b.   War and Property.

A further means beside community in work and language to strengthen the social impulses, is formed by the social development through the rise of war.

We have no reason to suppose that primitive man was a warlike being. Herds of ape men who gathered together in the branches of trees with copious sources of food can have squabbled and driven each other away. That this got so far as killing their opponents, of that there is no example among the living apes of today. Of male gorillas it is reported that they occasionally fight each other with such fury, that one kills the other, but that is a fight for a wife, not a fight for feeding grounds.

That changes so soon as man becomes a hunter, who has command of tools, which are directed in killing, and who has grown accustomed to killing, to the shedding of strange blood. Also another factor comes into account, which Engels has already pointed out to explain the cannibalism which often comes up at this period: the uncertainty of the sources of food. Vegetable food is in the tropical forest in abundance. On the grassy plains, on the other hand, roots and fruits are not always to be found, the capture of game is moreover for the most part a matter of chance.

The beasts of prey have thus acquired the capacity of being able to fast for incredibly long periods.   The human stomach has not such powers of endurance.   Thus necessity easily forces a tribe of savages to a fight for life or death with another neighboring tribe, which has got a good hunting territory; then the passions aroused by the fight and agonizing hunger finally drive him not simply to kill the foe but also to eat him.

In this way technical progress lets loose struggles, which the ape man did not know, fights not with animals of other kinds, but with the members of his kind themselves, struggles, often more bloody than those with the leopard and the panther, against which at least the bigger apes understand very well how to defend themselves when united in greater numbers.

Nothing is more fallacious than the idea that the progress of culture and increase of knowledge necessarily bring also higher humanity with them. We could far better say, the ape is humaner, therefore more human than man. Murder and slaughter in numbers of his species for economic motives are products of culture of technic in arms.   And up to now the perfection of these has ranked as a great part of the intellectual labor of mankind.

Only under special circumstances and in special

classes will there in the farther progress of culture be produced what we call the refinement of
manners. The progress in division of labor as-
signs the task of killing animals and man to certain classes — Hunters, Butchers, Executioners,
Soldiers, etc., who then occupy themselves with
brutality or cruelty either as a sport or as a business within the boundaries of civilization. Other
classes are entirely relieved of the necessity nay,
even the possibility of shedding blood, so for instance, the vegetarian peasants in the river val-
leys of India, who are prevented by nature from
keeping great herds of animals and for whom
the ox is too costly as a beast of burden or the
cow as a giver of milk for them to be in a position to kill them. Even the majority of the town
inhabitants of the European states since the decay of the town Republics and the rise of paid
armies as well as the rise of a special class of
butchers are relieved of the necessity to kill life.
Especially the intellectuals have been for centuries so unused to the spilling of blood, which they
ascribed to their higher intelligence, which roused
milder feelings in them. But in the last century
the universal military service has become again
a general institution of most European States
and the wars are again become people's wars,
and with that the refinement of manners among
our intellectuals has reached its end. They

have become since then considerably more brutal; the death penalty which even in the fifty years of last century was generally condemned, meets with no opposition any longer, and the cruelties of colonial wars, which fifty years ago at least in Germany would have made their authors impossible, are excused today — even glorified.

In any case war plays among modern peoples no more the same rôle as once among the nomadic pastoral and hunting tribes. But if it produces cruelty and bloodthirstiness on the one hand, it shows itself on the other as a powerful weapon to strengthen the bonds within the family, or society. The greater the dangers which threaten the individual, so much the more dependent does he feel himself from his society, his family, his class who alone with their joint forces can protect him. So much the greater the respect enjoyed by the virtues of unselfishness or a bravery which will risk life for the society. The more bloody the wars between tribe and tribe, the more will the system of selection have effect among them, those tribes will assert themselves best who have not only the strongest but also the cleverest, the bravest, the most self sacrificing and best disciplined members to show. Thus war works in primitive times in the most various manners to strengthen the social instincts in men. War, however, alters its forms in the course of the social evolution. Also its causes change.

Its first cause, the uncertainty of the sources of food, ceases so soon as agriculture and breeding of animals are more developed. But then begins a new cause of war: the possession of wealth. Not private property but the tribal property. Side by side with tribes in fruitful regions we find others in unfruitful; adjoining nomadic, water searching and poor shepherds, settled peasants to whom water has no longer value, whose farming produces plentiful surpluses, etc. War now becomes robbery and defense against robbery, and it has remained in essence the same till today.

Even this kind of war has a strengthening effect on the social instincts, so long as the property in the tribe is in the main communal. On the other hand the strengthening of the social instincts through war ceases to strengthen the social instincts the more classes are formed in the community, and war becomes more and more a simple affair of the ruling classes, whose endeavors are aimed towards an increase in their sphere of exploitation; or to put themselves in the place of another ruling class on a neighboring land. For the subject classes it is often enough in such wars no more about any question of their existence, and occasionally not even any question of a better or worse standard of life for them but only who is to be their lord. On the other hand, the army becomes either an aristocratic army, in which the mass of the people has no part, or where they co-operate it becomes a paid or a compulsory army, which is commanded by the ruling classes, and must put their lives at stake not for their own property, their own wives and children, but to champion the interests of others, often hostile interests. No more from social instincts but solely from fright for a remorselessly cruel penal code are such armies held together. They are divided by the hate of the mass against the leaders, by the indifference, even the mistrust of the latter against their subordinates.

At this stage war ceases to be for the mass of the people a school of social feelings. In the ruling, warrior classes it becomes a school of a haughty, overbearing demeanor towards the governed classes, because it teaches the ruling classes to treat the former just as they do the common soldiers in the army, to degrade them to blind subordination to an absolute commander and to dispose of their forces, nay, even their life without any scruples.

This development of war is as we have said already a consequence of the development of property, which again comes from the technical development.

Every object, which is produced in society or with which production is carried on in it must be at the disposal of some one and dispose of it can either a group or a single individual or the entire society. The nature of this disposal is determined in the first place by the nature of the things, and the nature of the method of production and that of the products. Who himself made his weapons, used them himself; just so who prepared himself a garment or an ornament; on the other hand it was equally natural that the house which was built by the common labor of the tribe should be inhabited in common by them. The various kinds of enjoyment of the various things for utility was always allowed, and repeated from generation to generation became the fixed customs.

Thus arose a law of custom, which was then extended still further in this way, that as often as quarrels arose over this method of all or about persons who had the right to all, the assembled members of the tribe decided. Law did not arise from any thought out legislation or social compact, but from a custom resting on the technical conditions, and where these did not suffice, on individual decisions of the society which decided each case by itself. Thus arose little by little a complicated right of property in the various means of production and products of society.

Common property, however, preponderated in the beginning, especially in the means of production, a soil worked in common, water apparatus, houses, even also herds of animals and other things besides. Even this common property was bound very largely to strengthen the social impulses, the interest in the common good, and also the subordination to the same and the dependence on the same.

Very differently did the private property of single families or individuals work out, so soon as it arrived at such a pitch that it began to usurp the place of common property. That began when in consequence of the growing division of labor the various branches of hand work began to separate themselves from agriculture in which they had hitherto found a by-employment; when they became more and more independent and separated into branches.

This development means an extension of the sphere of society through the division of labor, an extension of the number of those men who thereby form a society, because they work for each other and thus are mutually dependent for their existence on each other. But this extension of the social labor does not develop on the lines

of an extension of work in common, but towards
a separation of individuals from the common
work, and to making their work the private work
of independent producers who produce that
which they themselves do not consume, and obtain in return the products of other branches to
consume them.

Thus at this stage the common production
and common property in the means of production
of societies,(each in the main satisfying its own)
wants, for example, the mark or at least the
house community give way before the individual
production and property of single individuals or
pairs with their children, who produce commodities.   That is production not for their own use
but for sale, for the market.

With that there arises side by side with private
property, which had already existed at an earlier
period, even if not to so great an extent, an
entirely new element in society: the competitive
struggle of the different producers of the same
kind, who struggle against each other for their
share of the market.

War and competition are often regarded as
the only forms of the struggle for existence in the
entire natural world.   In fact both arise from
the technical progress of mankind and belong
to its special peculiarity.   Both are distinguished
from the struggle for existence of the animal

world therein, that the latter is a struggle of individuals or entire societies against the surrounding nature, a fight against living and non-living forces of nature in which those best fitted out for the particular circumstances could best maintain themselves and reproduce their kind. But it is no fight for life or death against other individuals of the same kind, with the exception of a few beasts of prey, even with whom, however, the last kind of struggle plays only a secondary part in the struggle for life, and with the exception of the struggle for the sexual natural selection. With man alone, thanks to the perfection of his tools, the struggle against individuals of the same kind to maintain themselves in the struggle for life comes to the fore. But even then there is a great distinction between wars and the struggle for existence. The first is a struggle which breaks out between two different societies; it means an interruption of production and this can never be a permanent institution. It presupposes, however, at least where no great class antagonisms exist, the strongest social cohesion and this encourages in the highest degree the social instincts. Competition on the other hand is a struggle between individuals, and indeed between individuals of the same society. This struggle is a regulator, certainly a most peculiar one, which keeps the social co-operation of the various individuals going, and arranges, that in the last resort these private producers shall always produce what is socially necessary. If war forms an occasional interruption of production, the struggle for existence, so does the struggle for life form its constant and necessary companion in the production of commodities.

Just as war so does competition mean a tremendous waste of force, but it is also a means to extort the highest degree of tension of all the productive forces and their most rapid improvement. It has consequently a great economic importance, till it creates such gigantic productive forces that the frame-work of commodity-production becomes too narrow, as one time the frame-work of the primitive social or co-operative production became too narrow for the growing division of labor. The overproduction not less than the artificial limitation of production by employers' associations, shows that the time is past when competition as a spur to production helps on social evolution.

But it has always done even this, only because it drove it on to the greatest possible expansion of production. On the other hand the competitive struggle between individuals of the same society has under all circumstances an absolutely deadly effect on the social impulses. Since in this struggle each one asserts himself so much the better the less he allows himself to be led by social considerations, the more exclusively he has his own interest in eye. For men under a developed system of production of commodities it seems only too clear that egoism is the only natural impulse in man, and that the social impulses are only a refined egoism or an invention of priests to get the mastery over man, or to be regarded as a supernatural mystery. If in society of today the social impulses have kept any strength, it is only due to the circumstance that general commodity production is only quite a young phenomenon, hardly 100 years old, and that in the degree in which the primitive democratic communism disappears and therewith war ceases to be a source of social impulses, a new source of the same breaks forth so much the stronger, the class war of the forwards struggling exploited classes of the people, a war not by paid soldiers, not by conscripts, but by volunteers, fought not for other people's interests but in the interests of their own class.

IV. THE INFLUENCE OF THE SOCIAL INSTINCTS.

a. Internationalism.

Far more than the degree of strength does the sphere in which the social instincts are effective alter itself. The traditional Ethics looked on the moral law as the force which regulates the relations of man to man. Since it starts with the individual and not with the society it overlooks the fact certainly that the moral law does not regulate the intercourse of men with every other man, but simply with men of the same society. That it only holds good for these will be comprehensible when we recollect the origin of the social instincts. They are a means to increase the social cohesion, to add to the strength of society. The animal has social instincts only for members of his own herd, the other herds are more or less indifferent to him. Among social beasts of prey we find direct hostility to the members of other herds. Thus the pariah dogs of Constantinople in every street look very carefully out that no other dog comes into the district. It would be at once chased away or even torn to pieces.

In a similar relation do the human herds come, so soon as hunting and war rise in their midst. One of the most important forms of the struggle for existence is now for them the struggle of the herd against other herds of the same kind. The man who is not a member of the same society becomes a direct enemy. The social impulses do not only not hold good for him but directly against him. The stronger they are, the better does the tribe hold together against the common foe, so much the more energetically do they fight the latter. The social virtues, mutual help, self sacrifice, love of truth, etc., apply only to fellow tribesmen not for the members of another social organization.

It excited much resentment against me when I stated these facts in the Neue Zeit and my statement was interpreted as if I had attempted to establish a special social democratic principle in opposition to the principles of the eternal moral law, which demands unconditional truthfulness to all men. In reality I have only spoken out that which has from the time when our forefathers became men lived as the moral law within our breasts, viz., that over against the enemy the social virtues are not required. There is no need, however, on that account that anybody should be especially indignant with the social democracy because there is no party which interprets the idea of society more widely than they, the party of internationalism, which draws all nations, all races into the sphere of their solidarity.

If the moral law applies only to members of our own society, its extent is still by no means fixed once for all. It grows far more in the same degree in which the division of labor progresses, the productivity of human labor grows as well as the means of human intercourse improve. The number of people increase whom a certain territory can support, who are bound to work in a certain territory for one another and with one another and who thus are socially tied together. But also the number of territories increase whose inhabitants live in connection with each other in order to work for each other and form a social union. Finally the range of the territories extends itself which enter into fixed social dependence on each other and form a permanent social organization with a common language, common customs, common laws.

After the death of Alexander of Macedonia the peoples of the Eastern Mediterranean had formed already an international circle with an international language, — Greek. After the rise of the Romans all the lands round the Mediterranean became a still wider international circle, in which the national distinctions disappeared, and looked upon themselves as the representatives of humanity.

The new religion of the circle which took the place of the old national religions, was from the very beginning a world religion with one God, who embraced the entire world, and before whom all men were equal. This religion applied itself to all mankind, and declared them all to be children of one God, all brothers.

But in fact the moral law held good even here only for the members of their own circle of culture, for " Christians," for " believers." And the centre of gravity in Christianity came ever more and more towards the north and west during the migration of the peoples. In the South and East there formed itself a new circle of culture with its one morality, that of Islam, which forced its way forward in Asia and Africa, as the Christian in Europe.

Now, however, this last expanded itself thanks to capitalism, ever and more to a universal civilization, which embraced Buddhists, Moslems, Parsees, Brahmans, as well as Christians, who more and more ceased to be real Christians.

Thus there formed itself a foundation for the final realization of that moral conception already expressed by Christianity, though very prematurely, so that it could not be fulfilled, and which thus remained for the majority of Christians a simple phrase, the conception of the equality of men, a view that the social instincts, the moral virtues are to be exercised towards all men in equal fashion. This foundation of a general human morality is being formed not by a moral improvement of humanity, whatever we are to understand by that, but by the development of the productive forces of man, by the extension of the social division of human labor, the perfection of the means of intercourse. This new morality is, however, even today far from being a morality of all men even in the economically progressive countries. It is in essence even today the moral of the class conscious proletariat, that part of the proletariat which in its feeling and thinking has emancipated itself from the rest of the people and has formed its own morality in opposition to the Bourgeoisie.

Certainly it is capital which creates the material foundation for a general human morality, but it only creates the foundation by treading this morality continually under its feet. The capitalist nations of the circle of European Society spread this by widening their sphere of exploitation which is only possible by means of force. They thus create the foundations of a future universal solidarity of the nations by a universal exploitation of all nations, and those of the drawing in of all colonial lands into the circle of European culture by the oppression of all colonial lands with the worst and most forcible weapons of a most brutal barbarism.

The proletariat alone have no share in the capitalist exploitation; they fight it and must fight it and they will on the foundation laid down by capital of world intercourses and world commerce create a form of society, in which the

equality of man before the moral law will become
— instead of a mere pious wish — reality.

b. The Class Division.

But if the economic development thus tends
to make wider the circle of society within which
the social impulses and virtues have effect till it
embraces finally the whole of humanity, it at the
same time creates not only private interests
within society which are capable of considerably
diminishing the effect of these social impulses,
for the time, but also special classes of society,
which while within their own narrow circle greatly intensifying the strength of the social instincts
and virtues, at the same time, however, can mate-
rially injure their value for the other members
of the entire society or at least for the opposing
sections or classes.

The formation of classes is also a product of
the division of labor. Even the animal society
is no homogeneous formation. In its bosom
there are already various groups, which have a
different importance in and for the community.
Yet the group-formation still rests on the natural
distinctions. There is in the first place that of
sex, then of age. Within each sex, we find the
groups of the children, the youths of both sexes,
the adults, and finally the aged. The discovery
of the tool has at first the effect of emphasizing

still more the separation of certain of these groups. Thus hunting and war fall to the men, who are more easily able to get about than the women, who are continually burdened with children. That and not any inferior power of self-defence probably it was which made hunting and fighting a monopoly of man. Wherever in history and fable we come across female huntresses and warriors, they are always the unmarried. Women do not lack in strength, endurance or courage, but maternity is not easily to be reconciled with the insecure life of the hunter and warrior. As, however, motherhood drives the woman rather to continually stay in one place those duties fall to her which require a settled life, the planting of field fruits, the maintenance of the family hearth.

According to the importance which now hunting and war, on the other side agriculture and domestic life attain for society, and according to the share which each of the two sexes has in these employments, changes the importance and relative respect paid to the man and woman in the social life. But even the importance of the various ages depends on the method of production. Does hunting preponderate, which renders the sources of food very precarious, and from time to time necessitates great migrations, the old people become easily a burden to the society.

They are often killed, sometimes even eaten. It is different when the people are settled; the breeding of animals and agriculture produce a more plentiful return. Now the old people can remain at home and there is no lack of food for them. Now is, however, at the same time a great sum of experiences and knowledge stored up, whose guardians, so long as writing was not discovered or become common property of the peoples are the old folk. They are the handers down of what might be called the beginning of science. Thus they are not now looked on as a painful burden, but honored as the bearers of a higher wisdom. Writing and printing deprive the old people of the privilege to incorporate in their persons the sum of all experiences and traditions of the society. The continual revolutionizing of all experience, which is the characteristic feature of the modern system of production, makes the old traditions even hostile to the new. The latter counts without any further ado as the better, the old as antiquated and hence bad. The old only receives sympathy, it enjoys no longer any prestige. There is now no higher praise for an old man than that he is still young and still capable of taking in new ideas.

As the respect paid to the sexes, so does the respect paid to the various ages alter in society with the various methods of production.

The progressive division of labor brings further distinctions within each sex, most among the
men. The woman is in the first place more and
more tied to the household, whose range dimin-
ishes, instead of growing, as ever more branches
of production break away from it, become independent and a domain of the men. Technical
progress, division of labor, the separation into
trades was limited till last century almost exclusively to men; the household and the woman
have been only slightly affected by these changes.

The more this separation into different professions advances, the more complicated does
the social organism become, whose organs they
form. The nature and method of their co-operation in the fundamental social process, with
other words the method of production, has nothing of chance about it. It is quite independent
of the will of the individuals, and is necessarily
determined by the given material conditions.
Among these the technical factor is again the most
important, and that phase whose development af-
fects the method of production. But it is not
the only one.

Let us take an example. The materialist conception of history has been often understood as
if certain technical conditions of itself meant a
certain method of production, nay, even certain
social and political forms. As that, however, is

not exact, since we find the same tools in various states of society, consequently the materialist conception of history is false and the social relations are not determined by the technical conditions. The objection is right, but it does not hit the materialist conception of history, but its caricature, by a confusion of technical conditions and method of production.

It has been said for instance, the plough forms the foundation of the peasant economy. But manifold are the social circumstances in which this appears!

Certainly! But let us look a little more closely. What brings about the deviations of the various forms of society which arise on the peasant foundations.

Let us take for example a peasantry, which lives on the banks of a great tropical or subtropical river, which periodically floods its banks, bringing either decay or fruitfulness for the soil. Water dams, etc., will be required to keep the water back here and to guide it there. The single village is not able to carry out such works by itself. A number of them must co-operate, and supply laborers, common officials must be appointed, with a commission to set the labor going for making and maintaining the works. The bigger the undertaking, the more villages must take a part, the greater the number of the forced laborers, the greater the special knowledge required to conduct such works, so much the greater the power, and knowledge of the leading officials compared with the rest of the population. Thus there grows on the foundation of a peasant economy a priest or official class as in the river plains of the Nile, the Euphrates or the Whang-Ho.

We find another species of development where a flourishing peasant economy has settled in fruitful, accessible lands in the neighborhood of robbers, nomadic tribes. The necessity of guarding themselves against these nomads forces the peasants to form a force of guards, which can be done in various manners. Either a part of the peasant applies itself to the trade of arms, and separates itself from the others who yield them services in return, or the robber neighbors are induced by payment of a tribute to keep the peace and to protect their new proteges from other robbers, or finally the robbers conquer the land and remain as lords over the peasantry, on whom they lay a tribute, for which, however they provide a protective force. The result is always the same: the rise of a new feudal nobility which rules and exploits the peasants.

Occasionally the first and second methods of development unite, then we have beside a priest and official class a warrior caste.

Again quite differently does the peasantry develop on a sea with good harbors, which favor sea voyages and bring them closer to other coasts with well to do populations. By the side of agriculture, fishery arises, fishery which soon passes over into sea-piracy and sea commerce. At a particularly suitable spot for a harbor is gathered together plunder and merchants' goods and there is formed a town of rich merchants. Here the peasant has a market for his goods, there arise for him money receipts, but also the expenditure of money, money obligations, debts. Soon he is the debtor of the town money proprietor.

Sea piracy and sea commerce as well as sea wars bring, however, a plentiful supply of slaves into the country. The town money owners instead of exploiting their peasant debtors any farther, go to work to drive them from their possessions, to unite these into great plantations, and to introduce slave work for peasant, without any change being required in the tools and instruments of agriculture.

Finally we see a fourth type of peasant development in inaccessible mountain regions. The soil is there poor and difficult to cultivate. By the side of the agriculture, the breeding of stock retains the preponderance; nevertheless both are not sufficient to sustain a great increase of population. At the foot of the mountains fruitful, well tilled lands tempt them. The mountain peasants will make the attempt to conquer these and exploit them, or where they meet with resistance to hire out their superfluous population as paid soldiers. Their experience in war, in combination with the poverty and inaccessibility of their land serves to guard it against foreign invaders, to whom in any case their poverty offers no great temptation. There the old peasant democracy still maintains when all around all the peasantry have long become dependent on Feudal Lords, Priests, Merchants and usurers. Occasionally a primitive democracy of that kind itself tyrannizes and explores a neighboring country which they have conquered, in marked contradiction to their own highly valued liberty. Thus the old cantons of the fatherland of William Tell exercised through their Bailiffs in Tessin in the seventeenth and eightcenth centuries a rule, whose crushing weight could compare with that of the mythical Gessler.

It will be seen that very different methods of production are compatible with the peasant economy. How are these differences to be explained? The opponents of the materialist conception of history trace them back to force, or again to the difference of the ideas which take form at various periods in the various peoples.

Now it is certain that in the erection of all

these methods of production force played a great part, and Marx called it the midwife of every new society. But whence comes this rôle of force, how does it come that one section of the people conquers with it, and the other not, and that the force produces this and not other results? To all these questions the force theory has no answer to give. And equally by the theory of ideas does it remain a mystery where the ideas come from which lead to freedom in the mountain country, to priest rule in the river valley land, to money and slave economy on the shores of the sea and in hilly undulating countries to feudal serfdom.

We have seen that these differences in the development of the same peasant system rest on differences in the natural and social surroundings in which this system is placed. According to the nature of the land, according to the description of its neighbors will the peasant system of economy be the foundation for very different social forms. These special social forms become then side by side with the natural factors, further foundations, which give a peculiar form to the development based on them. Thus the Germans found when they burst in on the Roman Empire during the migration of the peoples, the Imperial Government with its bureaucracy, the municipal system, the Christian Church as social conditions, and these, as well as they could, they incorporated into their system.

All these geographical and historical conditions have to be studied, if the particular method of production in a land at a particular time is to be understood. The knowledge of the technical conditions alone does not suffice.

It will be seen that the materialist conception of history is not such a simple formula as its critics usually conceive it to be. The examples here given show us, however, also how class differences and class antagonisms are produced by the economic development.

Differences not simply between individuals but also between individual groups within the society existed already in the animal world as we have remarked already, distinctions in the strength, the reputation, perhaps even of the material position of individuals and groups. Such distinctions are natural and will be hardly likely to disappear even in a socialist society. The discovery of tools, the division of labor, and its consequences, in short the economic development contributes still further to increase such difference or even to create new. In any case, they cannot exceed a certain narrow limit, so long as the social labor does not yield a surplus over that necessary to the maintenance of the members of the society. As long as that is not the case, no idlers can be maintained at the cost of society, none can get considerably more in social products than the other. At the same time, however, there arise [at this very stage owing to the increasing enmity of the tribes to each other and the bloody method of settling their differences, as well as through the common labor and the common property] so many new factors, through which the social instincts are strengthened that the small jealousies and differences arising between the families, the different degrees of age or the various callings can just as little bring a split in the community as that between individuals. Despite the beginnings of division of labor which are to be found there, human society was never more closely bound up together or more in unison than at the time of the primitive gentile co-operative society which preceded the beginning of class antagonisms.

The things, however, alter, so soon as social labor begins, in consequence of its necessary productivity, to produce a surplus. Now it becomes possible for single individuals and professions to secure for themselves permanently a greater share in the social product than the others can secure. Single individuals, only seldom temporarily and as a matter of exception will be able to achieve that for themselves alone; on the other hand it is very obvious that any class specially favored in any particular manner by the circumstances, for example such as are con- ferred by special knowledge or special powers of self defence, can acquire the strength to per- manently appropriate the social surplus for them- selves. Property in the products is narrowly bound up with property in the means of pro- duction, who possesses the latter can dispose of the former. The endeavors to monopolize the social surplus by the privileged class produce in it the desire to monopolize and take sole pos- session of the means of production. The forms of this monopoly can be very diverse, either com- mon ownership of the ruling class, or caste, or private property of the individual families or individuals of this class.

In one way or another the mass of the work- ing people becomes disinherited, degraded to slaves, serfs, wage laborers; and with the com- mon property in the means of production and their use in common is the strongest bond torn asunder which held primitive society to- gether.

And where the social distinctions which man- aged to form themselves in the bosom of primi- tive society kept within narrow limits, now the class distinctions which can form themselves have practically no limit. They can grow on the one side through the technical progress which increases the surplus of the product of the social labor over the amount necessary to the simple maintenance of society; on the other hand through the expansion of the community while the number of the exploiters remains the same or even decreases, so that the number of those working and producing surplus for each exploiter grows. In this way the class distinctions can enormously increase, and with them grow the social antagonisms.

In the degree in which this development advances society is more and more divided; the class struggle becomes the principal, most general and continuous form of the struggle of the individuals for life in human society; in the same degree the social instincts towards society as a whole lose strength, they become, however, so much the stronger within that class whose welfare is for the mass of the individuals always more and more identical with that of the commonweal.

But it is specially the exploited, oppressed and uprising classes in whom the class war thus strengthens the social instincts and virtues. And that because they are obliged to put their whole personality into this with much more intensity than the ruling classes, who are often in a position to leave their defence, be it with the weapons of war, be it with the weapons of the intellect, to hirelings. Besides that, however, the ruling classes are often deeply divided internally through the struggles between themselves for the social surplus and over the means of production. One of the strongest causes of that kind of division we have learnt in the battle of competition.

All these factors, which work against the social instincts, find none or little soil in the exploited classes. The smaller this soil, the less property that the struggling classes have, the more they are forced back on their own strength, the stronger do their members feel their solidarity against the ruling classes, and the stronger do their own social feelings towards their own class grow.

V. THE TENETS OF MORALITY.

a. *Custom and Convention.*

We have seen that the economic development introduces into the moral factors transmitted from the animal world an element of pronounced mutability, in that it gives a varying degree of force to the social instincts and virtues at different times; and also at the same time in different classes, that it, however, in addition widens and then again narrows down the scope within which the social impulses have effect, on the one side expanding its influence from the tiny tribe till it embraces the entire humanity, on the other side limiting it to a certain class within the society.

But the same economic development creates in addition a special moral factor, which did not exist at all in the animal world, and is the most changeable of all, since not only its strength but also its contents are subject to far reaching change. These are the *tenets of morality.*

In the animal world we find only strong moral feelings, but no distinct moral precepts which are addressed to the individual. That assumes that a language has been formed which can describe not only impressions but also things or at least actions, a language for whose existence in the animal world all signs fail, for which also a need first arises with the common work. Then is it possible to address distinct demands to the individual. Do these demands arise from individual and exceptional needs, then they will again disappear with the individual exceptional case. If on the other hand they have their origin in the social relations, they will revive again and again, so long as these relations last; and in the beginnings of society, where the development is very slow, one can allow hundreds of thousands of years for the endurance of particular social conditions. The social demands in the individual repeat themselves so often, and so regularly that they become a habit, of which the outline is finally inherited, as the tendency to peculiar kinds of hunting by the sporting dogs, so that certain suggestions suffice to arouse the habit in the descendants as well, also for instance the feeling of shame, the habit of covering certain portions of the body whose nude state appears immoral.

Thus arise demands on the individual in society, so much the more numerous, so much the more complicated it is, which demands finally by force of habit become without long consideration recognized as moral commands.

From this customary character many materialist Ethical writers have concluded that the entire being of morals rise alone on custom. With that it is nevertheless by no means exhausted. In the first place only such views become moral commands through habit which favor the consideration of the individual for the society, and regulate his conduct to other men. If it be brought against this, that there are individual vices which count as immoral, yet their original condemnation was certainly also in the interest of society. Thus for example, masturbation if general must prejudice the chance of securing a numerous progeny — and such a progeny appeared then when Malthus had not yet spoken, as one of the weightiest foundations of the well being and progress of society.

In the Bible (Genesis XXXVIII) Onan was killed by Jehovah, because he allowed his spermatazoa to fall to the ground instead of attending to his duty and having intercourse with the wife of his dead brother, so as to raise up seed for this latter.

The moral rules could only for this reason become customs because they met deep lying, ever returning social needs. Finally, however, a simple custom cannot explain the force of the feeling of duty, which often shows itself more powerful than all the instincts of self preservation. The customary element in morals only has the effect that certain rules are forthwith recognized as moral, but it does not produce the social instincts which compel the performance of already recognized moral laws.

Thus for example it is a matter of habit that counts it as disreputable, when a girl shows herself in her night gown to a man, even when this garment goes down to the feet, and takes in the neck, while it is not improper if a girl appears in the evening with a much uncovered bosom at a ball before all the world, or if she exhibits herself to the licentious gaze of men of the world at a watering place in a wet bathing gown. But only the force of the social instincts

can bring it about that a strongly moral girl
should at no price submit to that which conven-
tion, fashion, custom, in short society has once
stamped as shameful, and that she should occasionally even prefer death itself to that which
she regards as shame.

Other moralists have carried the idea of the
moral regulations as simple customs still farther
and described them as simple conventional fashions, basing this on the phenomenon that every
nation, nay, each class, has its own particular
moral conceptions which often stand in absolute
contradiction to each other, that consequently an
absolute moral law has no validity. It has been
concluded from that that morality is only a
changing fashion, which only the thoughtless
philistine crowd respect, but which the overman
can and must raise himself above as things
that appertain to the ordinary herd.

But not only are the social instincts something
absolutely not conventional, but something deeply
grounded in human nature, the nature of man as
a social animal; even the moral tenets are nothing arbitrary but arise from social needs.

It is certainly not possible in every case to fix
the connection between certain moral conceptions and the social relations from which they
arose. The individual takes moral precepts from
his social surroundings without being aware of

their social causes.   The moral law becomes then habit to him, and appears to him as an emanation of his own spiritual being, given a priori to him, without any practical root.   Only scientific investigation can gradually show up in a series of cases the relations between particular forms of society, and particular moral precepts, and then much remains dark.   The social forms, from which moral principles arose which still hold good at a later period, often lie far back, in very primitive times.   Besides that to understand a moral law, not only the social need must be understood which called it forth, but also the peculiar thought of the society which created it. Every method of production is connected not only with particular tools and particular social relations, but also with the particular content of knowledge, with particular powers of intelligence, a particular view of cause and effect, a particular logic, in short a particular form of thought.   To understand earlier modes of thought is, however, uncommonly difficult, much more difficult than to understand the needs of another or his own society.

All the same, however, the connection between the tenets of morals and the social needs has been already proved by so many practical examples, that we can accept it as a general rule. If, however, this connection exists then an alter-

ation of society must necessitate an alteration in
many moral precepts. Their change is thus not
only nothing strange, it would be much more
strange if with the change of the cause the effect
did not also change. These changes are necessary, for that very reason necessary because
every form of society requires certain moral
precepts suited to its condition. How diverse
and changing are the moral rules is well known.
Hence one example suffices to illustrate a morality differing from the present day European.

Fridtjof Nansen gives us in the tenth chapter
of his "Esquimaux Life" a very fascinating
picture of Esquimaux morals, from which I take
a few passages.

One of the most beautiful and marked features in the
character of the Esquimo is certainly their honorable-
ness. . . . For the Esquimo it has especial value
that he should be able to rely on his fellows and neighbors. In order, however, that his mutual confidence,
without which common action in the battle for life is
impossible, should continue, it is necessary that he
should act honorably to others as well. . . . For
the same reasons they do not lie readily to each other,
especially not the men. A touching proof of that is
the following incident related by Dalager: " If they have
to describe to each other anything, they are very careful
not to paint it more beautiful than it deserves. Nay,
if any one wants to buy anything which he has not seen,
the seller describes the thing, however much he may
wish to sell it, always as something less good than
it is."

The morals of advertising are unknown to the Esquimaux as yet. Certainly that applies to their intercourse with each other. To strangers they are less strict.

"Fisticuff fights and that sort of ruffianism is not to be seen among them. Murder is also a great rarity and where it happens is not a consequence of economic quarrels but of love affairs." They consider it dreadful to kill a fellowman. War is hence quite incomprehensible to them and abominable; their language has not even a word for it, and soldiers and officers who have been trained to the calling of killing people are to them simply butchers of men.

"Those of our commandments, against which the Greenlanders oftenest sin is the sixth. Virtue and chastity do not stand in great esteem in Greenland. Many look on it (on the west coast) as no great shame if an unmarried girl has children. While we were in Gothhael, two girls there were pregnant, but they in no way concealed it, and seemed from this evident proof that they were not looked down upon to be almost proud. But even of the east coast Holm says that it is there no shame if an unmarried girl has children."

"Egede also says that the women look on it as an especial bit of luck and a great honor, to have intimate connection with an Angekok, that is, one of their Prophets, and wise men, and adds — even many men are very glad and will pay the Angekok for sleeping with their wives, especially if they themselves cannot have children by them.

"The freedom of Esquimo women is thus very different to that appertaining to the Germanic women.

The reason certainly lies in the fact that while the maintenance of the inheritance, of the race and family has always played a great rôle by the Germans, this has no importance for the Esquimos because he has nothing to inherit, and for him the main point is to have children . . . ."

"We naturally look on this morality as bad. With that, however, is by no means said that it is so for the Esquimos. We must absolutely guard against condemning from our standpoint views which have been developed through many generations and after long experience by a people, however much they contradict our own. The views of good and bad are namely extraordinarily different on this earth. As an example I might quote, that when this Egede had spoken to an Esquimo girl of love of God and our neighbor, she said 'I have proved that I love my neighbor because an old woman who was ill and could not die, begged me that I would take her for a payment to the steep cliff, from which those always are thrown who can no more live. But because I love my people, I took her there for nothing and threw her down from the rocks.' "

"Egede thought that this was a bad act, and said that she had murdered a human being. She said no, she had had great sympathy with the old woman and had wept as she fell. Are we to call this a good or bad act?"

We have seen that the necessity of killing old and sick members of society very easily arises with a limited food supply and this killing becomes then signalized as a moral act.

"When the same Egede at another time said that God punished the wicked, an Esquimo said to him he also belonged to those who punished the wicked, since he had killed three old women who were witches.

"The same difference in the conception of good and bad is to be seen in regard to the sixth commandment. The Esquimo puts the commandment: 'Be fruitful and multiply' higher than chastity. He has every reason for that as his race is by nature less prolific."

Finally a quotation from a letter sent by a converted Esquimaux to Paul Egede who worked in the middle of the 18th century in Greenland as a missionary and found the Esquimaux morals almost untouched by European influence. This Eskimo had heard of the colonial wars, between the English and Dutch and expresses his horror over this inhumanity.

"If we have only so much food that we can satisfy our hunger and get enough skins to keep out the cold, we are contented, and thou thyself knowest that we let the next day look after itself. We would not on that account carry war on the sea, even if we could. . . . We can say the sea that washes our coasts belongs to us as well as the walruses, whales, seals and salmon swimming in it; yet we have no objection when others take what they require from the great supply, as they require it. We have the great luck not to be so greedy by nature as them. . . . It is really astonishing, my dear Paul! Your people know that there is a God, the ruler and guider of all things, that after this life they will be either happy or damned, according as they have

behaved themselves, and yet they live as though they
had been ordered to be wicked, and as if sin would
bring them advantage and honor. My countrymen
know nothing either of God or Devil and yet they behave respectably, deal kindly and as friends with each
other, tell each other everything and create their means
of subsistence in common.

It is the opposition of the morality of a primitive communism to capitalist morality which appears here. But still another distinction arises.
In the Eskimo society the theory and practice of
morality agree with one another; in cultivated
society a division exists between the two. The
reason for that we will soon learn.

b. The System of Production and Its Super-structure.

The moral rules alter with the society, yet
not uninterruptedly and not in the same fashion
and degree as the social needs. They become
promptly recognized and felt as rules of conduct
because they have become habit. Once they
have taken root as such they can for a long time
lead an independent life, while technical progress
advances, and therewith the development of the
method of production and the transformation of
the social needs goes on.

It is with the principles of morality as with
the rest of the complicated sociological superstructure which raises itself on the method of

production. It can break away from its foundation and lead an independent life for a time.

The discovery of this fact has overjoyed all those elements who could not escape the influence of the Marxian thought, but to whom nevertheless the consequences of the economic development are extremely awkward, who in the manner of Kant would like to smuggle in the spirit as an independent driving power in the development of the social organism. To these the discovery of the fact that the intellectual factors of society can temporarily work independently in it was very convenient. With that they hoped to have finally found the wished for reciprocal action — the economic factor works on the spirit and this on the economic factor, both were to rule the social development, either so that at one period the economic factor, at another again the spiritual force drives the society forwards, or in the manner that both together and side by side produce a common result, that in other words our will and wishes can at least occasionally break through the hard economic necessity of their own strength and can change it.

Undoubtedly there is a reciprocal action between the economic basis and its spiritual superstruction — morality, religion, art, etc. We do not speak here of the intellectual influence of inventions; that belongs to the technical conditions, in which the spirit plays a part by the side of the tool; technic is the conscious discovery and application of tools by thinking men.

Like the other ideological factors morality can also advance the economic and social development. Just in this lies its social importance. Since certain social rules arise from certain social needs they will render the social co-operation so much the more easy, the better they are adapted to the society which creates them.

Morality thus reacts on the social life. But that only holds good so long as it is dependent from the latter, as it meets the social needs from which it sprang.

So soon as morality begins to lead a life independent of society, so soon as it is no longer controlled by the latter, the reaction takes on another character. The further it is now developed the more is that development purely logical and formal. As soon as it is separated from the influence of the outer world it can no more create new conceptions, but only arrange the already attained ones so that the contradictions disappear from them. Getting rid of the contradictions, winning a unitary conception, solving all problems which arise from the contradictions, that is the work of the thinking spirit. With that it can, however, only secure the intellectual superstructure already set up, not rise superior

to itself. Only the appearance of new contradictions, new problems can affect a new development. The human spirit does not, however, create contradictions from out of its own inner being; they are produced in it only by the impress
of the surrounding world on it.

So soon as the moral principles grow independent they cease to be in consequence, an element of social progress. They ossify, become
a conservative element, an obstacle to progress.
Thus something can happen in the human society that is impossible in the animal; morality
can become instead of an indispensable social
bond, the means of an intolerable restraint on
social life. That is also a reciprocal action but
not one in the sense of our anti-materialist moralists.

The contradictions between distinct moral principles and distinct social needs can arrive at a
certain height in primitive society; they then
become, however, still deeper with the appearance of class antagonisms. If in the society
without classes, the adherence to particular moral
principles is only a matter of habit, it only requires for their supersedence that the force of
habit be overcome. From now on the maintenance of particular moral principles becomes a
matter of interest, often of a very powerful interest. And now appear also weapons of force,

of physical compulsion, to keep down the exploited classes, and this means of compulsion is
placed also at the service of " morality," to secure obedience to moral principles which are in
the interest of the ruling classes.

The classless society needs no such compulsory
weapons.   Certainly even in it the social instincts
do not always suffice to achieve the observance
by every individual of the moral code; the
strength of the social impulses is very different
in the different individuals, and just as different
that of the other instincts, those of self maintenance and reproduction.   The first do not always win the upper hand.   But as a means of
compulsion, of punishment, of warning, for
others, public opinion of the society, suffices in
such cases for the classless society.   This does
not create in us the moral law, the feeling of
duty.   Conscience works in us when no one sees
us and the power of public opinion is entirely
excluded; it can even under circumstances in a
society filled with class antagonisms and contra-
dictory moral codes force us to defy public opinion.

But public opinion works in a classless society
as a sufficient weapon of policy to secure the
public obedience to moral codes.   The individual
is so weak compared to society, that he has not
the strength to defy their unanimous voice.   This

has so crushing an effect, that it needs no further means of compulsion or punishment, to secure the undisturbed course of the social life. Even today in the class society we see that the public opinion of their own class or where that has been abandoned of the class or party which they form, is more powerful than the compulsory weapons of the state. Prison, poverty and death are preferred by people to shame.

But the public opinion of one class does not work on the opposite class. Certainly society can, so long as there are no class antagonisms in it, hold the individual in check through the power of its opinion and force obedience to its laws, when the social instincts in the breast of the individual do not suffice. But public opinion fails where it is not the individual against society but class against class. Thus the ruling class must apply other weapons of compulsion if they are to prevail, means of superior physical or economic might, of superior organization, or even of superior intelligence. To the soldiers, police, and judges are joined the priests as an additional means of rule, and it is just the ecclesiastical organization to whom the special task falls of conserving the traditional morality. This connection between religion and morality is achieved so much easier as the new religions which appear at the time of the decay of the primitive communism and the gentile society, stand in strong opposition to the ancient nature religions, whose roots reach back to the old classless period, and which know no special priest caste. In the old religions Divinity and Ethics are not joined together. The new religions on on the other hand grow on the soil of that philosophy in which Ethics and the belief in God are most intimately bound up together, the one factor supporting the other. Since then religion and Ethic have been intimately bound together as a weapon of rule. Certainly the moral law is a product of the social nature of man; certainly the moral code of the time is the product of particular social needs; certainly have neither the one nor the other anything to do with religion. But that kind of morals, which must be maintained for the people in the interests of the ruling class, that requires religion badly and the entire ecclesiastical organism for its support. Without this it would soon go to pieces.

Old and New.

The longer, however, the outlived moral standards remain in force, while the economic development advances and creates new social needs, which demand new moral standards, so much the greater will be the contradiction be-

tween the ruling morals of society and the life
and action of its members.

But this contradiction shows itself in the different classes in different manners. The conservative classes, those whose existence rests on
the old social conditions, cling firmly to the old
morality. But only in theory. In practice they
cannot escape the influence of the new social
conditions. The well known contradiction between moral theory and practice begins here.
It seems to many a natural law of morals; that
its demands should be something desirable but
unrealizable. The contradiction between theory
and practice in morality can, however, here again
take two forms. Classes and individuals full of
a sense of their own strength ride roughshod
over the demands of the traditional morality,
whose necessity they certainly recognize for others. Classes and individuals which feel themselves weak, transgress secretly against the moral
codes, which they publicly preach. Thus this
phase leads according to the historical reiteration
of the decaying classes either to cynicism or
hyprocrisy. At the same time, however, there
disappears, as we have seen, very early in this
very class the power of the social instincts in
consequence of the growth of private interests,
as well as the possibility of allowing their place
in the coming battles to be taken by hirelings

wherever they avoid entering personally into the fray.

All that produces in conservative, or ruling classes, more phenomena which we sum up as immorality.

Materialist moralists, to whom the moral codes are simple conventional fashions, deny the possibility of an immorality of that kind as a social phenomenon. As all morality is relative, that which is called immorality is simply a deviating kind of morality.

On the other hand idealist moralists conclude from the fact that there are entire immoral classes and societies that there must be a moral code eternal and independent of time and space; a standard independent of the changing social conditions on which we can measure the morals of every society and class.

Unfortunately, however, it is that element of human morality which, if not independent of time and space is yet older than the changing social relations, the social instinct, is just that which the human morality has in common with the animal. What, however, is specifically human in morality, the moral codes, is subject to continual change. That does not prove all the same, that a class or a social group cannot be immoral, it proves simply that so far at least as the moral standards are concerned, there is just as little an absolute morality as an absolute immorality. Even the immorality is in this respect a relative idea. Only the lack of mere social impulses and virtues, which man has inherited from the social animals, is to be regarded as absolute immorality.

If we look on the other hand on immorality as an offence against the laws of morality, then it implies no longer the divergence from a distinct standard, holding good for all times and places, but the contradiction of the moral practice to its own moral principles, it implies the transgression against moral laws which people themselves recognize and put forward as necessary. It is thus nonsense to declare particular moral principles of any people or class, which are recognized as such, to be immoral simply because they contradict our moral code. Immorality can never be more than a deviation from our own moral code, never from a strange one. The same phenomenon, say of free sexual intercourse or of indifference to property can in one case be the product of moral depravity, in a society where a strict monogamy and the sanctity of property are recognized as necessary; in another case it can be the highly moral product of a healthy social organism which requires for its social needs neither property in a particular woman nor that in particular means of consumption and production.

d. The Moral Ideal.

If, however, the growing contradiction between the changing social conditions and the stagnating morality of the conservatives, that is, the ruling classes, tends to growing immorality and shows itself in an increase of hypocrisy and cynicism, which often goes hand in hand with a weakening of the social impulses, so does it lead to quite other results in the rising and exploited class. Their interests are in complete antagonism to the social foundation, which created the ruling morality. They have not the smallest reason to accept it, they have every ground to oppose it. The more conscious they become of their antagonism to the ruling social order, the more will their moral indignation grow as well, the more will they confront to the old traditional morality a new moral, which they are about to make the morality of society as a whole. Thus comes up in the uprising classes a moral ideal, which grows ever bolder, the more they win in strength. And at the same time, as we have already seen, the power of the social instincts in the same classes will be especially developed by means of the class struggle so that with the daring of the new moral ideal the enthusiasm for the same also

increases. Thus the same evolution which produces in conservative or down going classes increasing immorality produces in the rising classes
a mass of phenomena which we sum up under
the name of ethical idealism, which is not, however, to be confused with the philosophical idealism. The very uprising classes are indeed often
inclined to philosophical materialism which the
declining class oppose from the moment when
they become conscious that reality has spoken the
sentence of death over them and feel that they
can only look for salvation from supernatural
powers divine or ethical.

The content of the new moral ideal is not
always very clear. It does not emerge from any
scientific knowledge of the social organism, which
is often quite unknown to the authors of the
ideal, but from a deep social need, a burning
desire, an energetic will for something other than
the existing, for something which is the opposite
of the existing. And thus also this moral ideal
is fundamentally only something purely negative,
nothing more than opposition to the existing
hypocrisy.

So long as class rule has existed, the ruling
morality has guarded wherever a sharp class antagonism has been formed, slavery, inequality,
exploitation. And thus the moral ideal of the
uprising classes in historical times has always had

the same appearance, always that which the French Revolution summed up with the words, Freedom, Equality, and Fraternity. It would seem as if this was the ideal implanted in every human breast independent of time and space, as if this were the task of the human race to strive from its beginning for the same moral ideal, as if the evolution of man consisted in the gradual approach to this ideal which continually looms before them.

But if we examine more closely, we find that the agreement of the moral ideal of the various historical epochs is only a very superficial one and that behind there lie great differences of social aims, which correspond to the differences of the social situation at the time.

If we compare Christianity, the French Revolution, the Social Democracy today we find that Liberty and Equality for all meant something quite different according to their attitude towards property and production. The primitive Christians demanded equality of property in the manner that they asked for its equal division for purpose of consumption by all. And under Freedom they understood the emancipation from all work as is the lot of the toilers of the field who neither toil nor spin and yet enjoy their life.

The French Revolution again understood by equality, the equality of property rights. Private property it declared to be sacred. And true freedom was for it the freedom to apply property in economic life, according to pleasure in the most profitable manner.

Finally the Social Democracy neither swears by private property nor does it demand its division. It demands its socialization, and the equality which it strives for is the equal rights of all in the products of social labor.

Again the social freedom which it asks for is neither freedom to dispose arbitrarily of the means of production and to produce at will, but the limitation of the necessary labor through the gathering in of those capable of working and through the most extended application of labor-saving machinery and methods. In this way the necessary labor which cannot be free but must be socially regulated can be reduced to a minimum for all and to all a sufficient time assured of freedom, for free artistic and scientific activity, for free enjoyment of life. Social freedom — we do not speak here of political — through the greatest possible shortening of the period of necessary labor: that is freedom as meant by the social democracy.

It will be seen that the same moral ideal of Freedom and Equality can embrace very different social ideals. The external agreement of the moral ideals of different times and countries is, however, not the result of a moral law independent of time and space, which springs up in man from a supernatural world, but only the consequence of the fact that despite all social differences the main outlines of class rule in human society have always been the same.

All the same a new moral ideal cannot simply arise from the class antagonism. Even within the conservative classes there may be individuals who develop with their class socially only loose ties and no class consciousness. With that, however, they possess strong social instincts and virtues, which makes them hate all hypocrisy and cynicism, and they dispose of a great intelligence which shows them clearly the contradiction between the traditional moral code and the social needs. Such individuals are bound also to come to the point of lifting up the new moral ideal. But whether this new ideal shall obtain social force, depends upon whether they result in class ideals or not. Only the motive power of the class struggle can work fruitfully on the moral ideal. Because only the class struggle and not the single handed endeavors of self interested people possesses the strength to develop society farther and to meet the needs of the higher developed method of production. And so far as the moral ideal can in any degree be realized it can be attained only through an alteration of society.

A peculiar fatality has ruled hitherto that the moral ideal should never be reached. That will be easily understood when we consider its origin. The moral ideal is nothing else than the complex of wishes and endeavors which are called forth by the opposition to the existing state of affairs. As the motor power of the class struggle is a means to collect the forces of the uprising classes to the struggle against the existing and to spur them on, it is a powerful lever in the overturning of this existing. But the new social conditions, which come in the place of the old, do not depend on the form of the moral ideal but from the given material conditions, the technical conditions, the natural milieu, the nature of the neighbors and predecessors of the existing society, etc.

A new society can thus easily diverge a considerable way from the moral idea of those who brought it about, so much the more the less the moral indignation was allied with knowledge of the material conditions. And thus the ideal ended continually with a disillusionment; proving itself to be an illusion after it had done its historical duty and had worked as an impulse in the destruction of the old.

We have seen above how in the conservative classes the opposition between moral theory and practice arises, so that morality appears to them as that which everybody demands but nobody practices, something which is beyond our strength, what it is only given to supernatural powers to carry out. Here we see in the revolutionary classes a different kind of antagonism arise between moral theory and practice; the antagonism between the moral ideal and the reality created by the social revolution. Here again morality appears as something which everybody strives for but nobody obtains — as in fact the unattainable for earthly beings. No wonder that then the moralists think that morality has a supernatural origin and that our animal being which clings to the earth is responsible for the fact that we can only gaze wistfully at its picture from afar without being able to arrive at it.

From this heavenly height morality is drawn down to earth by the historical materialism. We make acquaintance with its animal origin and see how its changes in human society are conditioned by the changes which this has gone through, driven on by the development of the technic. And the moral ideal is revealed in its purely negative character as opposition to the existing moral order, and its importance is recognized as the motor power of the class struggle as a means to collect and inspire the forces of the revolutionary classes. At the same time, however, the moral ideal will be deprived of its power to direct our policy. Not from our moral ideal, but from distinct material conditions does the policy depend which the social development takes. These material conditions have already at earlier periods to a certain extent determined the moral will, the social aims of the uprising classes, but for the most part unconsciously. Or if a conscious directing social knowledge was already to hand, as in the 18th century, it worked all the same unsystematically and not consistently at the formation of the social aims.

It was the materialist conception of history which has first completely deposed the moral ideal as the directing factor of the social evolution, and has taught us to deduce our social aims solely from the knowledge of the material foundations. And with that it has shown for the first time the way through which it can be avoided, that the revolutionary reality should not come up to the social ideal, how illusions and disappointments are to be avoided. Whether they can be really avoided depends upon the degree of the insight acquired into the laws of development and of the movements of the social organism, its forces and organs.

With that the moral ideal will not be deprived of its influence in society; this influence will simply be reduced to its proper dimensions. Like the social and the moral instinct, the moral ideal is not an aim but a force or a weapon in the social struggle for life; the moral ideal is a special weapon for the peculiar circumstances of the class war.

Even the Social Democracy as an organization of the Proletariat in its class struggle cannot do without the moral ideal, the moral indignation against exploitation and class rule. But this ideal has nothing to find in scientific socialism, which is the scientific examination of the laws of the development and movement of the social organism, for the purpose of knowing the necessary tendencies and aims of the proletariat class struggle.

Certainly in Socialism the student is always a fighter as well, and no man can artificially cut himself in two parts, of which the one has nothing to do with the other. Thus even with Marx occasionally in his scientific research there breaks through the influence of a moral ideal. But he always endeavors and rightly to banish it where he can. Because the moral ideal becomes a source of error in science, when it takes it on itself to point out to it its aims. Science has only to do with the recognition of the necessary. It can certainly arrive at prescribing a shall, but this dare only come up as a consequence of the insight into the necessary.   It must decline to discover a " shall " which is not to be recognized as a necessity founded in the world of phenomena.   The Ethic must always be only an object of science; this has to study the moral instincts as well as the moral ideals and explain them; it cannot take advice from them as to the results at which it is to arrive.   Science stands above Ethics, its results are just as little moral or immoral as necessity is moral or immoral.

All the same even in the winning and making known scientific knowledge morality is not got rid of.   New scientific knowledge implies often the upsetting of traditional and deeply rooted conceptions which had grown to a fixed habit.   In societies which include class antagonisms, new scientific knowledge, especially that of social conditions, implies in addition, however, damage to the interests of particular classes. To discover and propagate scientific knowledge which is incompatible with the interests of the ruling classes, is to declare war on them.   It assumes not simply a high degree of intelligence, but also ability and willingness to fight as well as independence from the ruling classes, and before all a strong moral feeling : strong social instincts, a ruthless striving for knowledge and to spread the truth with a warm desire to help the oppressed uprising classes.

But even this last wish has a misleading tendency if it does not play a simple negative part, as repudiation of the claims of the ruling conceptions to validity, and as a spur to overcoming the obstacles which the opposing class interests bring against the social development but aspires to rise above that and to take the direction laying down certain aims which have to be attained through Social Study.

Even though the conscious aim of the class struggle in Scientific Socialism has been transformed from a moral into an economic aim it loses none of its greatness. Since what appeared to all social innovaters hitherto as a moral ideal, and what could not be attained by them, for this the economic conditions are at length given, that ideal we can now recognize for the first time in the history of the world as a necessary result of the economic development, viz.: the abolition of class. Not the abolition of all professional distinctions. Not the abolition of division of labor, but certainly the abolition of all social distinctions and antagonisms which arise from the private property in the means of production and from the exclusive chaining down of the mass of the people in the function of material production. The means of production have become so enormous, that they burst today the frame of private property. The productivity of labor is grown so huge that today already a considerable diminution of the labor time is possible for all workers. These grow the foundations for the abolition not of the division of labour, not of the professions, but for the antagonism of rich and poor, exploiters and exploited, ignorant and wise.

At the same time, however, the division of labor is so far developed as to embrace that territory which remained so many thousands of years closed to it, the family hearth. The woman is freed from it and drawn into the realm of division of labor, so long a monopoly of the men. With that naturally the natural distinctions do not disappear which exist between the sexes; it can also allow many social distinctions, as well as many a distinction in the moral demands which are made to them to continue to exist or even revive such, but it will certainly make all those distinctions disappear from state and society which arise out of the fact that the woman is tied down to the private household duties and excluded from the callings of the divided labor. In this sense we shall see not simply the abolition of the exploitation of one class by another, but the abolition of the subjection of woman by man.

And at the same time world commerce attains such dimensions, the international economic relations become so close that therewith the foundation is laid for superseding private property in the means of production, the overcoming of national antagonisms, the end of war, and armaments, and for the probability of permanent peace between the nations.

Where is such a moral ideal which opens such splendid vistas? And yet they are won from sober economic considerations and not from intoxication through the moral ideals of freedom, equality and fraternity, justice, humanity!

And these outlooks are no mere expectations of conditions which only ought to come, which we simply wish and will, but outlooks at conditions which must come, which are necessary. Certainly not necessary in the fatalist sense, that a higher power will present them to us of itself, but necessary, unavoidable in the sense, that the inventors improve technic and the capitalists in their desire for profit revolutionize the whole economic life, as it is also inevitable that the workers aim for shorter hours of labor and higher wages, that they organize themselves, that they fight the capitalist class and its state, as it is inevitable that they aim for the conquest of political power and the overthrow of capitalist rule. Socialism is inevitable because the class struggle and the victory of the proletariat is inevitable.

Printed in Great Britain by
Amazon.co.uk, Ltd.,
Marston Gate.